Bizarre Fantasy Rugby XV's

Having recently applied my expansive vocabulary (picked up in friendly discourse with opposition players on the rugby pitch) to my autobiography, I imagined that the phone would be ringing off the wall by now with eager publishers wishing to invest in my purple prose. No such luck. The only call I get is from this shower, asking me to introduce this new book of dodgy rugby teams. What's worse, I'm actually in it – and while I'm happy to be in the Moments Of Genius XV, I'm not quite so keen on the 'I Don't Fancy Yours Much' line-up. I mean, I might not be in the supermodel league, but I'm no Neil Jenkins either!

Oh well, that's rugby. You can't have it all (unless you're Jerry Guscott). So have a laugh on us, but be warned – the first person who calls me Hippo to my face had better be a bloody fast mover…

Keep smiling

John Bentley

JOHN BENTLEY

Bizarre Fantasy Rugby XV's

BY NICK BROWNLEE
AND DAVID KOHN

generation

The 'Bizarre Fantasy' series was created by David Kohn

GENERATION PUBLICATIONS
Editor Phil McNeill
Design Paul Sudbury, Generation Studio
Research Mark Crossland
Publications Manager Eve Cossins
Publishers David Crowe and Mark Peacock

Thanks to Joseph Crowe, Ailsa Jensen, Catherine Killingworth and Anna Skinner

All photographs courtesy of Allsport
with special thanks to Justin Davies

First published in Great Britain in 2000 by
Generation Publications
9 Holyrood Street
London SE1 2EL
Tel: 020 7 403 0364
genpub@btinternet.com

CIP data for this title is available from the British Library
ISBN 1 903009 29 4

Printed by Carmont Press Ltd, South Kirkby, West Yorkshire (01977 640262)
Distributed by Macmillan, MDL Sales Division (01256 302692)

BIZARRE TEAMS WHO PLAY WITH ODD-SHAPED BALLS

FOREWORD BY MICK 'THE MUNCH' SKINNER

Rugby union is a weird and wonderful game played by wild animals and supported by some game birds. Yes – it's a jungle out there!

From an early age at Blaydon Rugby Club, Tyne and Wear, I was taught that the Fat Boys were the forwards and the Pretty Boys were the backs, and it was imperative that these two halves of the XV stayed apart. In fact, as a forward, the main aim was NOT to give it to the backs – unlike today, when it seems the Girls have to get it at every opportunity. (No, I don't mean the female supporters and a good shagging, I mean the backs and the ball.) So the real men upfront strive to produce good quick ball for the skirts – though it's funny how it's never the right type of ball. I remember when any ball was good ball for the backs!

These Gel Boys are an important part of the team, of course. Without them there would be little flair and few tries. But all great teams need to have the right blend of peculiar individuals. There will always be a place in my team for that Bizarre player: the one who makes the difference. Rugby is all about the characters – and this book is a celebration of that.

Best Wishes
Mick Skinner

Just don't mess my hair up

Who said David Sole's talking out of his arse?

Hey, don't use all the hot water

Don't say Argentina are crap again

FAT BOYS, AND THE

PRETTY BOYS PLAIN BIZARRE

They're all here – just come on in...

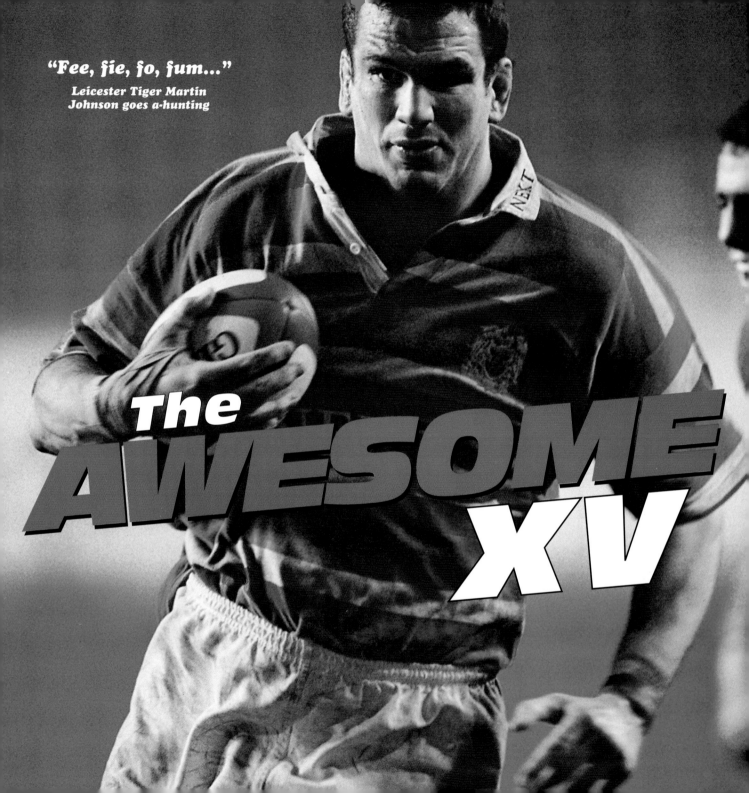

The AWESOME XV

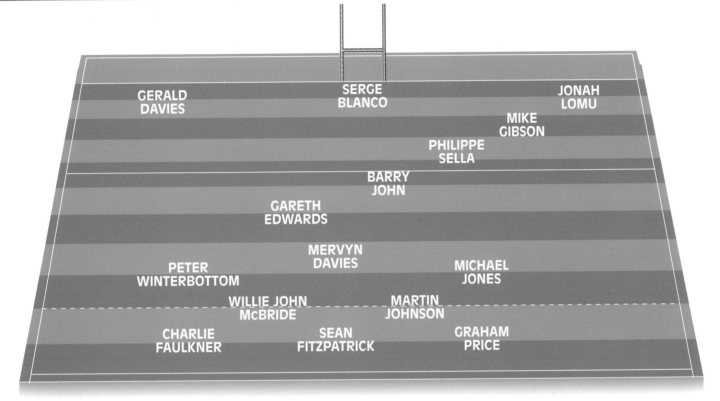

GERALD DAVIES

SERGE BLANCO

JONAH LOMU

MIKE GIBSON

PHILIPPE SELLA

BARRY JOHN

GARETH EDWARDS

MERVYN DAVIES

PETER WINTERBOTTOM

MICHAEL JONES

WILLIE JOHN McBRIDE

MARTIN JOHNSON

CHARLIE FAULKNER

SEAN FITZPATRICK

GRAHAM PRICE

I f rugby was all about up-and-unders, scrums and line-outs, there is no way you'd ever get 70,000 people packed into the great arenas such as Twickenham, Stade de France, Newlands and the Millennium Stadium. Rugby is about players – and what keeps us flocking to the big matches is the chance to see at first hand those players who have reached such heights as to become legendary.

These are the superstars whose deeds will continue to be passed down through rugby folklore long after they have hung up their boots. The players who, when their names are mentioned over a pint in clubhouses the world over, can only be described as … AWESOME.

"Après vous!" Blanco waves Fitzpatrick through during the 1987 World Cup Final

Serge calls over the tobacconist at half-time

FULL BACK
SERGE BLANCO

Like some laid-back jazz musician, Serge Blanco of France spent his time on the pitch exuding cool. A dedicated 40-a-day smoker, there is no doubt he would have puffed away on his beloved Gauloise fags during the boring bits in play – had the rules allowed. But, like the virtuoso he was, Blanco could blow 'em away whenever he stepped into the spotlight. His genius was his unpredictability. He could appear from anywhere in the backs, and his loping running style belied sizzling pace. Against England at Twickenham in 1991, it was Blanco's audacious run from behind his own posts that set up one of the great Five Nations tries. In the World Cup semi-final of 1987 against Australia, Blanco sealed a magnificent performance with a last-gasp try in the corner. Just two sensational moments from a glittering career.

WING
JONAH LOMU

"He's a freak," wailed white-faced Will Carling after Jonah Lomu had single-handedly trampled England out of the 1995 World Cup with four semi-final tries. Indeed, when Lomu's on the charge, even rugby's hardest nuts start thinking about taking up fishing. Mike Catt, England full back that fateful day in Cape Town, is no mean tackler – but Lomu simply ran over the top of him in Tom and Jerry style to get to the line. Rob Andrew and Tony Underwood were splattered en route. His performance turned Lomu into rugby's first global superstar. But soon after, his career was threatened with kidney problems. Typically, the big man fought back to become even more powerful, and it was like the return of a nightmare for England in the 1999 World Cup as Lomu smashed his way for 40 yards and through five flailing tackles to score a crucial try in the pool match at Twickenham. The "freak" was back.

"Long after the match, when the stadium was dark, we all went out on to the pitch. We did a lap of honour, and we sang! We sang Basque songs for half an hour. There was absolutely no one else there. Just us. It was our little secret. So happy, so proud of what we had done. Yes, the happiest men in the world."
– SERGE BLANCO on the French jubilation after they beat Australia 30-24 in the dramatic 1987 World Cup semi-final

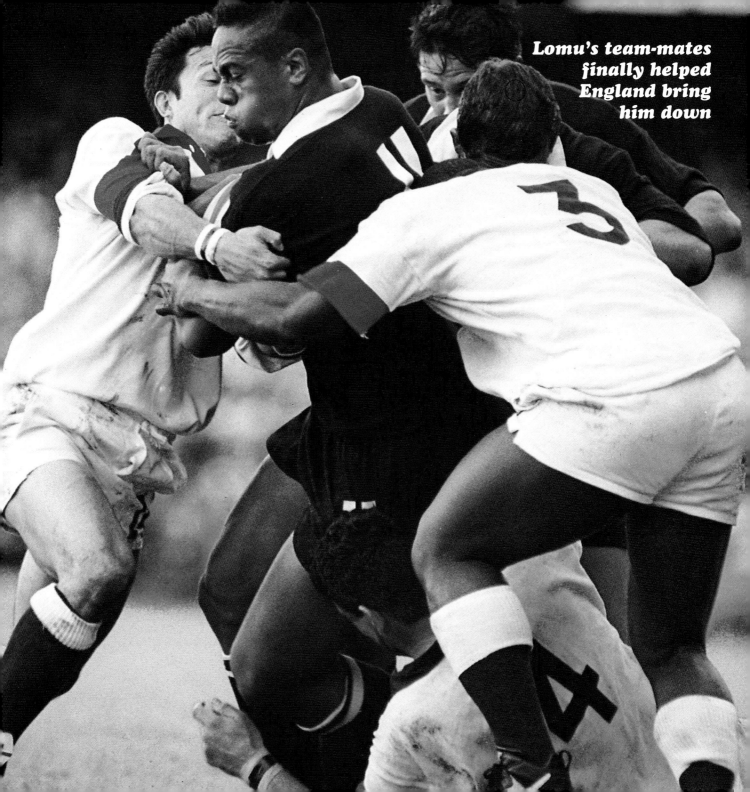

Lomu's team-mates finally helped England bring him down

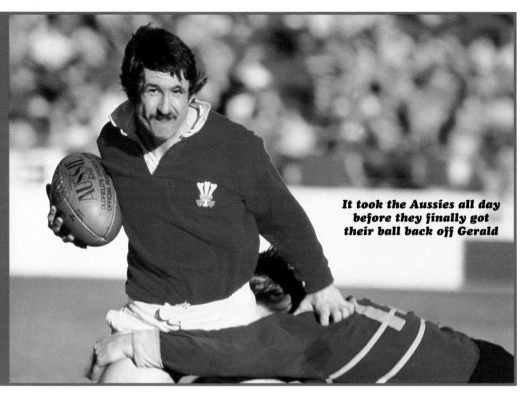

"Each sportsman needs to pit his wits against the best his day has to offer. Each competitor, however much he may yearn for peace and solitude in a distant dressing room when the heat of combat is about to begin and that strange nervous fatigue engulfs him, knows that he has to be there. The World Cup is such a testing arena; the final rugby frontier. I would like to have had a go."
– *GERALD DAVIES*
in his book
World Cup: Rugby's Battle Of The Giants
(Generation Publications)

It took the Aussies all day before they finally got their ball back off Gerald

WING
GERALD DAVIES

In the days before guile gave way to brute force, Gerald Davies was king of the wing. During Wales' glorious 1970s, Davies was the world's most devastating finisher. He began his international career in the centre, but was soon switched to the wing where, with his searing pace and bamboozling sidestep, he formed the cutting edge of a brilliant Welsh back line that included Barry John, Gareth Edwards, JJ Williams and JPR Williams. A legend of British rugby's golden era, Davies scored vital tries for the Lions in the historic series triumph in New Zealand.

CENTRE
MIKE GIBSON

Rock hard in the tackle and elusive in attack, Ireland's Mike Gibson was possibly the greatest all-round footballer the game has ever known. Just watch him in action for the Barbarians against New Zealand in 1973. Although he wasn't involved in the try, his quicksilver thinking and movement proceeded to cut the mighty Blacks to ribbons for the rest of the game. Originally a fly half, he switched to centre with devastating effect. In 1974, he was the architect of Ireland's Grand Slam, scoring two tries in the 26-21 triumph over England. When

he retired in 1979, he was the most-capped player in the world with 69 appearances – still an Irish record.

CENTRE
PHILIPPE SELLA

Like all the greats, Philippe Sella was blessed with deceptive pace and startling vision. He was the backbone of the all-conquering French team of the 1980s, providing electrifying attacking options with bonecrunching defence. Against England in 1987, there seemed little danger as Richard Hill threw a speculative pass to his half-back partner Rob Andrew. Sella was on to it in a flash, plucking the ball out of the air and setting off on a weaving, pigeon-toed run to the line 65 metres away. England's cover tacklers were left grasping at air. The crucial score, typical of Sella's genius, clinched a Grand Slam.

FLY HALF
BARRY JOHN

It's unlikely the waif-like Welshman Barry John would last 10 minutes against today's ferocious man-mountain back-row forwards. For those 10 minutes, however, you could guarantee King John would take the breath away with his array of kicking skills and his will-o'-the-wisp running. Paired with Gareth Edwards, John was the finest exponent of the fly half's art. Quick, elusive, tactically brilliant, he was the architect of the Welsh glory years and of the Lions' win in New Zealand. He retired at 27, at the peak of his powers, and who knows what he might have achieved had he carried on?

SCRUM HALF
GARETH EDWARDS

It is no coincidence that two of the world's greatest fly halves – Barry John and Phil Bennett – played behind Gareth Edwards. With his long pass, his bravery in the tackle and his bullocking runs, Edwards gave his outside half more than enough time to work their magic. In a glittering career he won three Grand Slams, five Triple Crowns and five Five Nations championships, as well as starring for the Lions in 1971 and 1974. He scored many memorable tries, but it is the one against the All Blacks in 1973, when he dived over to complete a sensational seven-man move, that etched him into legend.

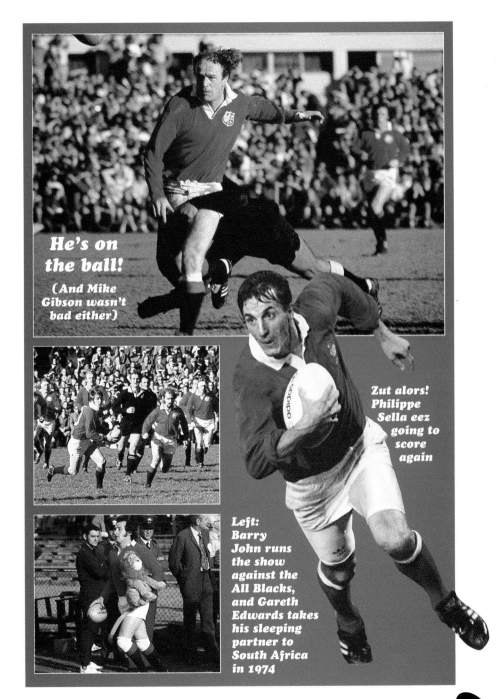

He's on the ball!
(And Mike Gibson wasn't bad either)

Zut alors! Philippe Sella eez going to score again

Left: Barry John runs the show against the All Blacks, and Gareth Edwards takes his sleeping partner to South Africa in 1974

In the '70s the Welsh front row could always take time out for a quick photo session while playing England

Graham Price, Bobby Windsor and Charlie Faulkner – otherwise known as the Viet Gwent

PROPS
GRAHAM PRICE
CHARLIE FAULKNER

Looking as if they had been hewn from the side of a Welsh mountain, Price and his front-row colleague Faulkner made up two thirds of a fearsome trio for Pontypool, Wales and the British Lions.

In an era of lumbering forwards, Price was a rarity – fit, athletic and mobile. His moment of glory came in 1975 against France at Parc des Princes. On a horrible, muddy pitch Price led an unlikely breakout from his own line and, when the ball popped up at the other end, he was on hand to fall over the line and score. As Nigel Starmer-Smith commented: "They'll never believe it in Pontypool!"

With Price at tighthead and Faulkner at loose, Wales won two Grand Slams and two Triple Crowns. Although never as mobile as Price, Faulkner had faultless technique and tireless strength which provided the solid platform for the array of talent outside the scrum.

HOOKER
SEAN FITZPATRICK

When New Zealand skipper Andy Dalton was injured on the eve of the 1987 World Cup, his replacement in the front row was the young Sean Fitzpatrick. For the next 10 years, Fitzpatrick and the All Blacks were to become an unstoppable force in world rugby. A fearsome competitor, if anyone summed up the single-minded desire of the All Blacks to succeed it was their nuggety captain.

Fitzpatrick played an unprecedented 63 consecutive Tests in the cauldron of the front row, a record broken only when he was rested from a pool game during the 1995 World Cup. It took him 11 years and 91 Tests before he finally missed an international through injury – and this was the knee problem which eventually brought this front row giant's brilliant career to a close. Although he never lifted the World Cup, he remains one of the All Blacks' most successful skippers.

**'You take Mickey Skinner,
I'll take Rob Andrew.'**

Sean Fitzpatrick shows the leadership
qualities that enabled him to make
91 Test appearances without an injury

SECOND ROW
MARTIN JOHNSON

England skipper Martin Johnson dominates the murky world of the line-out like no other player in world rugby. Indeed, Johnson is suspiciously good – lacking only a bolt through his neck to complete the appearance of a monster specially created from the bodies of long-dead line-out specialists. As captain of the victorious Lions team in South Africa in 1997 – one of most physical touring parties ever to leave these shores – Johnson led from the front, preferring to let his actions on the pitch do the talking.

FLANKER
PETER WINTERBOTTOM

England flanker Peter Winterbottom (below) didn't say much – but he did his talking on the pitch. In an often flaky England side, it was "Wints" who held things together with his tireless rampaging.

He saved some of his greatest performances for the 1983 Lions tour to New Zealand where, in an outclassed side, it seemed he was playing the Blacks on his own. Such is his appetite for the game that you'll still find him turning out in Golden Oldies tournaments, and showing the youngsters a trick or two.

FLANKER
MICHAEL JONES

Aged just 22, New Zealand's flying flanker Michael Jones found fame in the 1987 World Cup, thanks to his extraordinary ability, and his refusal to play on a Sunday because of his religious beliefs – which cost him a semi-final place.

It was fortunate indeed for the All Blacks that the final was played on a Saturday – because Jones was awesome. One French player later said he thought there had been three Michael Joneses on the pitch because wherever he looked, the All Black was there. He scored the first

SECOND ROW
WILLIE JOHN McBRIDE *(Captain)*

There may have been better second-row forwards than Willie John McBride – but never a better leader of men on and off the pitch. Whether captaining Ireland or the Lions, McBride was a towering presence whose easy-going, pipe-sucking manner hid a core of flint.

In South Africa in 1974, his now-infamous "99" call may have resulted in pitch battles, but it also showed the Springboks that the Lions were not to be bullied. After the final Test, having steered his team through the series unbeaten, McBride retreated to his hotel room for a contemplative smoke of his pipe. He was disturbed in the early hours by the hotel manager, who informed him that some of the Lions had set fire to the dining room and the police were on their way. Dressed only in his underpants, and with his pipe belching smoke, McBride asked: "How many police, exactly?"

McBride was despondent to see another ice-cream man flee when he ordered a 99

try and set up another, and his tackling rendered the flashy French impotent. Indisputably the best player in the world, his career was sadly curtailed by injury.

NO. 8
MERVYN DAVIES

With his trademark head bandage and '70s sideburns, Welsh skipper Mervyn Davies was the vital link between Wales's powerful forwards and their skilful backs.

Tall and rangy, Davies was dubbed "Merv the Swerve" for his habit of picking the ball from the back of the scrum and jinking his way through opponents. A Lions hero of 1974, Merv was capped 38 times for Wales and won eight of his nine games as captain. Just weeks after leading his country to a Grand Slam in 1976, however, Merv suffered a brain haemorrhage during a club match and was forced to retire from the game.

Plenty of beef, a bit too much pork, but definitely no chicken

Aye, it's a strange recipe that goes into a dish like Fran Cotton

The 'I DON'T FANCY YOURS MUCH' XV

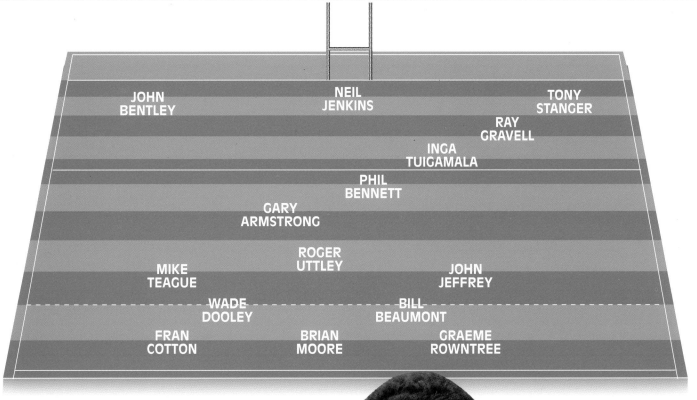

JOHN BENTLEY NEIL JENKINS TONY STANGER

RAY GRAVELL

INGA TUIGAMALA

PHIL BENNETT

GARY ARMSTRONG

ROGER UTTLEY

MIKE TEAGUE JOHN JEFFREY

WADE DOOLEY BILL BEAUMONT

FRAN COTTON BRIAN MOORE GRAEME ROWNTREE

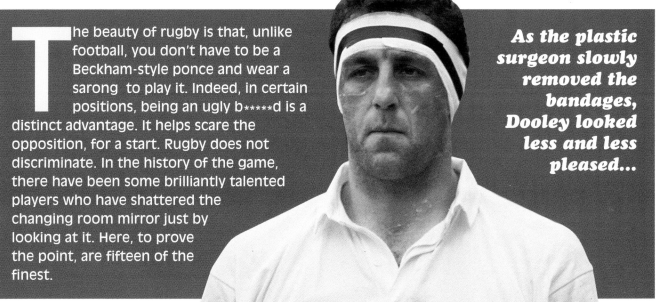

The beauty of rugby is that, unlike football, you don't have to be a Beckham-style ponce and wear a sarong to play it. Indeed, in certain positions, being an ugly b*****d is a distinct advantage. It helps scare the opposition, for a start. Rugby does not discriminate. In the history of the game, there have been some brilliantly talented players who have shattered the changing room mirror just by looking at it. Here, to prove the point, are fifteen of the finest.

As the plastic surgeon slowly removed the bandages, Dooley looked less and less pleased...

19

'Hey, boyo, I am not uglier than Phil Bennett'

FULL BACK
NEIL JENKINS

"Jenks" is the world's leading points scorer – but that's unlikely to cut much ice with the chicks in the nightclubs of Pontypridd. For, while he was blessed with a golden boot, the Welsh kicking machine was also cursed with thinning ginger hair, FA Cup ears and a face like a well-wellied Gilbert. Jenks slots the vital penalties, but it's noticeable that not many of his team-mates rush to give him a hug.

WING
TONY STANGER

Tony Stanger broke England hearts when he scored the decisive try in the 1990 Calcutta Cup match. But hey, what's worse – losing a rugby match or looking like you just got hit in the face with a bag of five pences? Like his snooker-playing Scottish chum Stephen Hendry, poor old Tony has never shaken off that teenage acne. Match-winning wingman, certainly – but no flower of Scotland.

WING
JOHN BENTLEY

Bentos scored one of the great tries for the Lions in South Africa. But few could blame the Gauteng defence for running a mile as the grimacing Tyke launched himself towards them. Clearly taking ugly lessons from the low-lifes he used to lock up as a copper in Leeds, Bentos decided to compound his already bag-of-spanners visage with a skinhead cut. Some would call that ungentlemanly conduct.

CENTRE
VA'AIGA TUIGAMALA

Like the crash-bang-wallop impact player he is, Inga the Winger smashes his way into our team of revolting rugby players. It's one thing to see the Samoan-turned-All Black-turned-Samoan pulling hideous faces during the Haka; it's quite another to realise that is actually what he looks like. Inga has taken the sheep shears to his hair and now looks even more like Oddjob – but twice as deadly.

CENTRE
RAY GRAVELL

Centres were traditionally clean-cut pretty boys. Then, in the '70s, came Ray Gravell of Wales. With Steve Fenwick, Gravell took centre play to previously unimagined depths of furry-faced, hairy-arsed brick-shithousedom. It was no surprise that England's backs annually shrivelled at the sight. Gravell paved the way for the likes of Devereux and Gibbs – but even they sidestepped the idea of sporting a ginger beard. Ray now commentates on TV – where mercifully you can't see his face.

FLY HALF
PHIL BENNETT

Wales not only produces the greatest fly halves, they also breed the ugliest. With his fellow countryman Neil Jenkins ensconced at full back, the No. 10 shirt goes to 1970s legend Phil Bennett. In his pomp, Phil could sidestep anything that moved – as the 1973 All Blacks would attest. But Benny's flattened features tell of how, as a young player learning his trade in the school of hard knocks, he obviously received one hand-off too many.

The crowd were surprised to see the hippo emerge with a rugby ball

Is it Desperate Dan? No, it's John Bentley

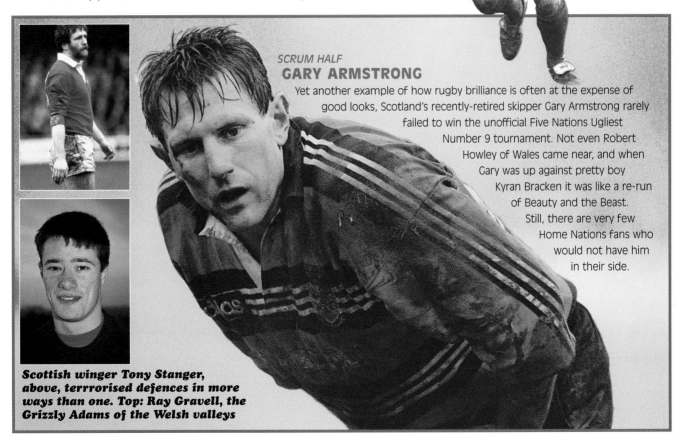

SCRUM HALF
GARY ARMSTRONG

Yet another example of how rugby brilliance is often at the expense of good looks, Scotland's recently-retired skipper Gary Armstrong rarely failed to win the unofficial Five Nations Ugliest Number 9 tournament. Not even Robert Howley of Wales came near, and when Gary was up against pretty boy Kyran Bracken it was like a re-run of Beauty and the Beast. Still, there are very few Home Nations fans who would not have him in their side.

Scottish winger Tony Stanger, above, terrrorised defences in more ways than one. Top: Ray Gravell, the Grizzly Adams of the Welsh valleys

'Well it's a one for the money...'

Moore's Elvis impression did not impress

FRONT ROW
FRAN COTTON
BRIAN MOORE
GRAEME ROWNTREE

A trio of England players make up our front row pug-uglies – and also make a case for the scrum being permanently packed down and out of sight. Lantern-jawed Fran Cotton was a colossus for England and the Lions. He not only played like a cornerstone, he looked like one too. Big Fran seemed to spend half his career with his face covered in mud. Most people agreed it was a vast improvement.

Cotton's 1980 Grand Slam hooker Peter Wheeler made a strong run for our team, but the honour goes to Brian Moore, who played with such distinction in the 1990s. By day, he was Mr Moore, respected solicitor. But on the pitch, with his toothless snarl, he became Pitbull, terror of rival packs and of any TV viewer who happened to tune in to an England match by mistake.

The other English rose at prop is Graeme Rowntree – the definitive example of why mums should not let their sons play rugby. His ears have been so mangled by his front-row chores that they're not so much cauliflower as a whole serving of vegetables. With his bogbrush hairstyle, Rowntree is the archetypal prop – and one of the best.

SECOND ROW
BILL BEAUMONT
WADE DOOLEY

Until recently you've never had to be much of an oil painting to play in the boilerhouse position of lock forward. Some of the ugliest rugger buggers ever to pick up the oval ball have emerged from the second row – where, to be fair, they have the most unenviable job in the game of grasping a prop's b****cks and shoving their head between two sweaty backsides. Despite scouring the globe for suitable candidates, however, we have had no option but to return to England for our selection.

Billy Beaumont was an inspirational captain both for his country and the Lions, and he remains one of the game's nice guys. Unfortunately, his Play-Doh face always made him look as if he'd packed down between one pair of arses too many.

Beaumont's backside was, in itself, quite remarkable, nay legendary, in the game. When topless Erika Roe raced on to the Twickenham pitch during a game against Australia, scrum half Steve Smith observed: "Hey Bill – there's a bird with your arse on her chest!"

When Beaumont was succeeded in the England boilerhouse by Wade Dooley, it was a rare example of England selectorial continuity.

Not only was Dooley a Lancastrian and a top line-out jumper, he was also phenomenally ugly. It was often suggested that, as a policeman, the Lurch-like Dooley should not be seen in built-up areas after the hours of darkness.

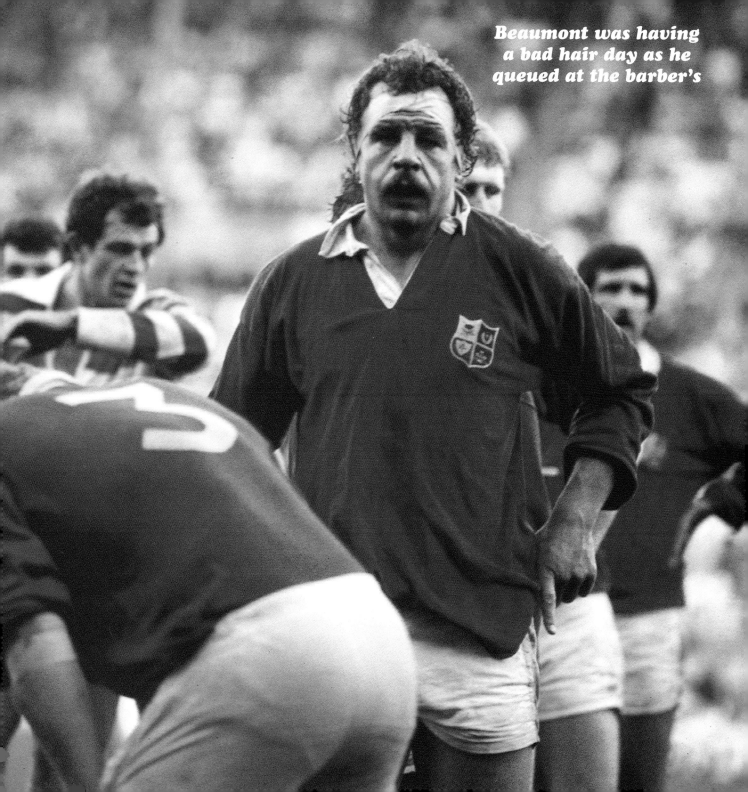

Beaumont was having a bad hair day as he queued at the barber's

And the winner of this week's beauty contest is ... the ball

Winterbottom, Teague, Leonard and Ackford – not recommended viewing for opponents of a nervous disposition

FLANKER
MIKE TEAGUE

Hewn from a slab of Gloucester granite, the Mighty Mike Teague made up a highly unpleasant-looking English back row featuring such kiddies' night-mares as Mick Skinner and Dean Richards. To his credit, Teague did attempt to disguise his appearance with a trendy 'tache and mullet combo so favoured by Home Nations players of the mid-'80s – but sadly it was never going to be enough. Instead, he covered himself with glory during the Lions tour to Australia in 1989 and in the World Cup in 1991. Mighty indeed.

Kids never took to the one-eyed Teletubby

Graeme Rowntree, nicknamed Wiggy (it's the ears)

'I bet this 'tache and long hair make me look really cool'

Roger Uttley in 1977

FLANKER
JOHN JEFFREY

Scotland's John Jeffrey was known as The White Shark. A more accurate description might have been The Red Nose. As icy February gales lashed Murrayfield, Jeffrey's conk stuck out like a belisha beacon as he tore around the pitch in search of victims to tackle, like Peter Schmeichel on speed. A hardy Borders farmer, Jeffrey's otherwise pasty-white visage was as battered as a Harry Ramsden cod.

NO. 8
ROGER UTTLEY
(Captain)

"Craggy" is the polite response to England hero Uttley's extraordinary mug. "Bloody hell!" is more common. Brave to a fault, Roger made a point of putting his face where most players kept their boots. The result was a bashed-up nose, boxer's brows and more stitches than the Bayeux Tapestry. It did not make for pleasant viewing – but then Uttley's total commitment did not make life pleasant for opponents either.

The PRETTY BOYS XV

BEN
TUNE

PERCY
MONTGOMERY

IEUAN
EVANS

JEREMY
GUSCOTT

THOMAS
CASTAIGNÈDE

JONNY
WILKINSON

JOOST VAN DER
WESTHUIZEN

NICK
JEAVONS

JEAN-PIERRE
RIVES

BOBBY
SKINSTAD

GARATH
ARCHER

JOHN
EALES

—

—

PHIL
KEARNS

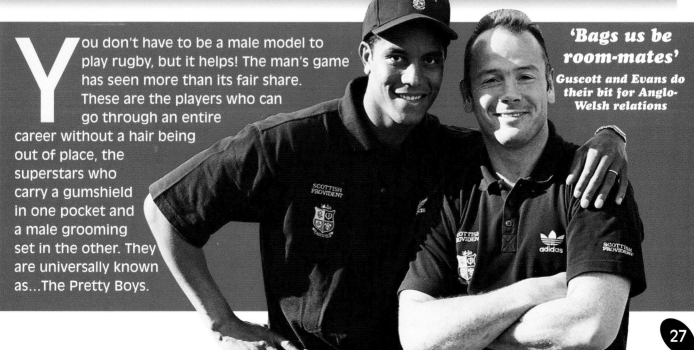

You don't have to be a male model to play rugby, but it helps! The man's game has seen more than its fair share. These are the players who can go through an entire career without a hair being out of place, the superstars who carry a gumshield in one pocket and a male grooming set in the other. They are universally known as...The Pretty Boys.

'Bags us be room-mates'
Guscott and Evans do their bit for Anglo-Welsh relations

27

WING
IEUAN EVANS

After a dodgy start in which he sported a football-style mullet hairdo, Welsh wizard Ieuan Evans cut off the surplus locks to become a fully-fledged member of the Pretty Boys. His good looks are more rugged than most, and with personal injuries and a decade of presiding over dismal Welsh performances, Ieuan has won a reputation as a bit of a moody b*****d. But on the odd occasion when he shows his beaming smile, he is a real ladykiller.

Adonis of the Valleys
— Ieuan Evans,
sex god and
*moody b * * * * d*

FULL BACK
PERCY MONTGOMERY

Had South Africa's André Joubert not sported a highly suspect Village People moustache, he would have easily taken this position. However his successor, Percy Montgomery, is the real deal. Blond, broad-shouldered and standing at well over 6ft, Montgomery looks like Adonis in a Springbok shirt. And not a 'tache or a construction worker's helmet in sight.

WING
BEN TUNE

Beach bum Ben could have stepped straight from the set of Neighbours. Australia's strapping winger is a try-scoring sensation – but you get the impression he would be equally at home with a surf board or grilling some prawns on the barbie. Shaving his hair down to a skinhead No.1 has only made the dear boy look like a 12-year-old.

CENTRE
JEREMY GUSCOTT

Judging by the modelling assignments and appearances on Gladiators, England's pretty boy Jerry Guscott is well aware of the earning potential of his remarkably unscathed looks. Combined with sublime skill, it's no wonder that even hairy-arsed England fans at Twickenham frequently shout out that they want his babies.

CENTRE
THOMAS CASTAIGNÈDE

If there was a Little Boys XV, then peroxide Thomas Castaignède of France would be skipper. After his winning drop goal against England, he cheekily stuck out his tongue – stirring the derision of men and the maternal instincts of women everywhere.

FLY HALF
JONNY WILKINSON

When Wilko was crunched by a Fijian tackle during the World Cup, it outraged mums around the world. The fact that "little" Jonny weighs in at over 14 stone and actually enjoys crash-tackling forwards twice his size is irrelevant to those who think he's a little cutie-pie from the first form who still carries conkers in the pockets of his shorts.

Ben Tune – even with a skinhead haircut he's a sweetie

'Can I go now, Clive? My mum says it's tea time'

SCRUM HALF
JOOST VAN DER WESTHUIZEN

Good looking and brilliant at rugby – South Africa's Joost van der Westhuizen makes you sick. He's the type of bloke who would not only score the winning try against your team, but score with your girlfriend in the nightclub later that night.

PROPS

Sadly, there are absolutely no props who qualify for the Pretty Boys XV.

HOOKER
PHIL KEARNS

Even up to his enforced retirement in 1999, Australian skipper Phil Kearns was almost freakishly untouched by a career on rugby's front line. His boyish good looks and full, gleaming white smile are quite extraordinary among international hookers. If you don't agree, then bear in mind that the next best-looking No. 2 on our list was Keith Wood of Ireland!

SECOND ROW
GARATH ARCHER

The fact that increasing numbers of forwards – including England's Garath Archer – have taken to wearing scrum caps suggests that a) they have been told to by their mums or b) they want to keep their faces nice for future modelling assignments. A rugged, blond-haired Geordie, pretty boy Archer would probably deny both.

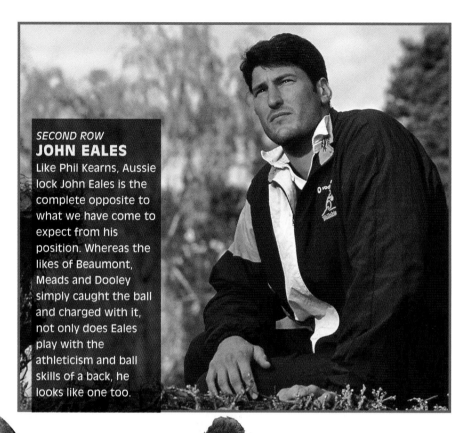

SECOND ROW
JOHN EALES

Like Phil Kearns, Aussie lock John Eales is the complete opposite to what we have come to expect from his position. Whereas the likes of Beaumont, Meads and Dooley simply caught the ball and charged with it, not only does Eales play with the athleticism and ball skills of a back, he looks like one too.

FLANKER
JEAN PIERRE RIVES

Watching old footage of French hero Jean Pierre Rives (left), you'd be forgiven for thinking his shoulder-length locks were red not blond, as he so often ended up covered in blood. Yet he managed to retain his dashing good looks despite going in where the studs were flying. For ladies who like the Braveheart look, this is your man. Now a sculptor, Monsieur Rives is rugby's answer to Bardot.

No.8
NICK JEAVONS (Captain)

In the dim, dark 1980s, England supporters had little to laugh about. Apart from Nick Jeavons (left), the original rugby pretty boy. Socks rolled down, shorts pulled up tight, Duran Duran hair flowing in the Twickenham breeze, Jeavons would stand like a Greek god beneath England's posts as yet another opposition conversion flew over his head. Utterly hopeless as a player, he nonetheless paved the way for the Skinstads and Guscotts – for which we are eternally grateful.

FLANKER
BOBBY SKINSTAD

The jury may be out as to whether South Africa's Bobby Skinstad is a great player – but there is no doubt that when it comes to looks, he is guilty of being Bobby Beautiful. Tanned, with strangely waxed legs, Skinstad recently crashed his car – although the rumour that he was gazing longingly at himself in the rear-view mirror at the time has yet to be proven.

Bobby performed rather better on the beach than in the World Cup

"The South African Rugby Union World Cup guide has eight pages on Bobby and two pages on other players. They want to make money out of his image. But the team still needs to win."
– *GARY TEICHMANN*
Ex-Springboks captain who was dropped for Bobby. And no, they didn't win

Battle of the Mullets!
Mick the Munch skins the Champ

HANDBAGS

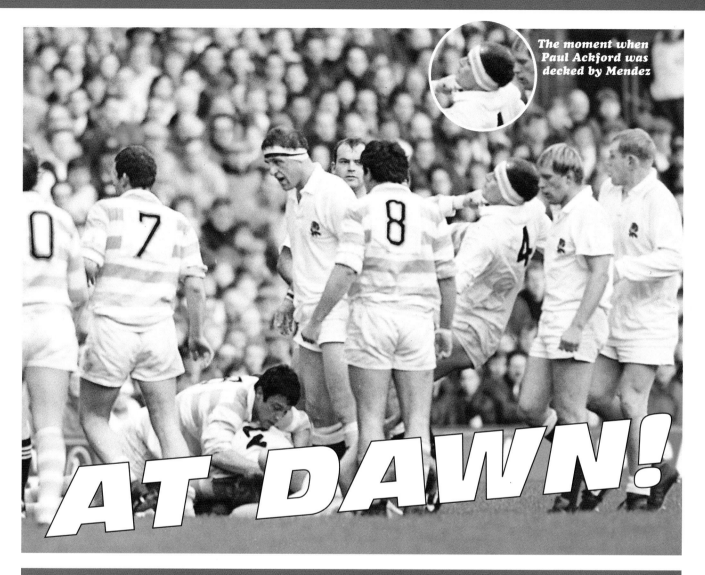

The moment when Paul Ackford was decked by Mendez

AT DAWN!

Commentators Bill McLaren and Nigel Starmer-Smith might call it disgraceful, but secretly everyone knows that rugby would not be the same game without its share of scrapping. Quite simply, it's a bit of harmless fun. Whereas stamping on somebody's head is not only premeditated and potentially disfiguring, nobody has ever been seriously hurt by a flailing fist in the middle of a mass brawl consisting of all 30 players. Like great tries, rugby fans savour the great haymakers and all-out barneys from down the years. Here is a selection of some of the finest.

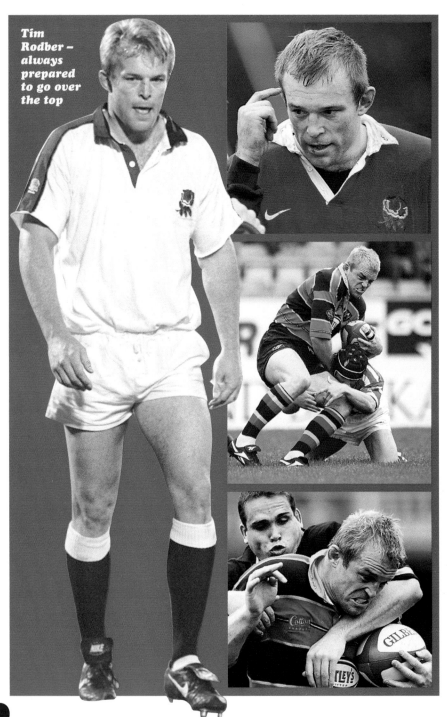

Tim Rodber – always prepared to go over the top

RODBER'S REVENGE
Rodber v Western Province

An ill-tempered match during England's 1994 tour to South Africa exploded in fine style, with acting skipper Tim Rodber playing a starring role. The catalyst was a vicious stamp on Jon Callard, which left the England full back with an ugly gash on his face. Army officer Rodber saw red, and set about ensuring retribution with a series of deadly uppercuts and hooks on whichever member of the Western Province side happened to hove into view. The result? Nobody was hurt and Rodber was sent off. But he remained unmoved by his actions. "I don't advocate what I did," he said later, "but someone had to do something. If I had seen Callard's face, I think I would have led the team off the field."

RODBER STRIKES AGAIN
Rodber v Popplewell

England's 46-6 romp over the Irish at Lansdowne Road in 1997 was enlivened by a bout of mass fisticuffs in which Tim Rodber was once again in the thick of the action. As with most brawls, this one started innocently enough with Irish prop Nick Popplewell getting a little frisky with his fists as a scrum broke up in disarray. Suddenly, all hell broke loose as the green and the white shirts began pounding away at each other. From five yards away, Rodber spotted something he didn't like and leapt in to deliver his now trademark combination on the head of Popplewell. Bizarrely, the only person the referee saw fit to caution was England's Richard Hill, who had been doing nothing more than attempting to break up the brawl.

THE BATTLE OF BALLYMORE

Burton v Osborne

This game between England and Australia in 1975 was famed for the dismissal of Mike Burton – the first English player to be sent off. But if there is any defence at all for Burton it is that he must have thought he was appearing in a WWF bout rather than a rugby match.

The handbags were drawn from the very first kick off. As England caught the ball, they were also caught by a torrent of flailing Aussie fists and boots.

A huge brawl erupted, involving all the players and cheered on by an enthusiastic home crowd.

The fight cooled down after several minutes, but kicked off again almost immediately. It was after two 15-a-side scraps that the hapless Burton took matters into his own hands and late-tackled Aussie winger Dave Osborne. The rest is history.

ACKFORD KNOCKED OUT BY A SCHOOLBOY

Mendez v Ackford

It was the mother of all punches – a sweeping right hook from 18-year-old Argentine prop Federico Mendez – that felled veteran England second row and police inspector Paul Ackford like a sack of hammers at Twickenham in 1990.

Mendez was sent off. Ackford, his legs wobbling like Bambi on ice, had to be helped from the pitch.

But Mendez's haymaker was merely the icing on a foul play cake which began at the scrum immediately before. As the scrum collapsed, Mendez found himself lying on the wrong side. England's Jeff Probyn accidentally stepped on him – which provoked Mendez to reach up and grab Probyn's testicles. Understandably this time, Probyn stood on the Argentine with more feeling.

Mendez got up and let fly at the nearest England player, which just happened to be the entirely innocent Ackford.

Ackford is helped off after being poleaxed by Mendez

SACRÉ BLEU!

Dubroca v Bishop

The 1991 World Cup quarter-final between France and England was a brutal affair which England narrowly won 19-10. French coach Daniel Dubroca (inset) was so incensed by what he regarded as unfair treatment by the officials that he cornered New Zealand referee David Bishop in the tunnel after the match and unleashed a stream of abuse in which he called Bishop a cheat. He then allegedly manhandled the official.

The French Federation claimed that Dubroca's English was not good enough to "abuse the referee seriously", and that his alleged strong-arm tactics were nothing but a "fraternal gesture". Dubroca was cleared – but resigned soon afterwards.

A FRIENDLY FRACAS WITH A FIJIAN

Jones v Naituivau

During a match between Cardiff and Fiji in Wales in 1992, the talented tourists were racing through for a try when the referee's attention was drawn to a brawl taking place miles away on the other side of the pitch. Chief protagonists were Cardiff's Derwyn Jones (left) and Fiji's monolithic prop Naituivau, who had been happily thumping away at each other for a good two or three minutes before being spotted by the official. Amazingly, both escaped with only a sound ticking-off.

If you can't catch the ball, just catch anything...

McBride's infamous 99 call kept the Lions on top of the Springboks

"99"

Lions v South Africa

The Lions tour to South Africa in 1974 was a triumph not only for British rugby but for British brawling. Following the tour to New Zealand in 1971, where Sandy Carmichael was brutally smashed in the face during a match against Canterbury, skipper Willie John McBride decided that the Lions would never again be used as Pommie punchbags. With his most able lieutenants, McBride devised the now infamous "99" call, in which all 15 players were encouraged to join in any punch-up.

Using this one-in-all-in tactic, McBride not only hoped to discourage the South Africans from picking on individuals, but also to prevent individual Lions being sent off for retaliation. It worked a treat: the all-out brawl in the First Test was a delight to behold, with punches flying, bodies toppling, but nobody isolated enough to be given their marching orders – although JPR Williams (below), who ran fully 20 yards in order to welly a South African, was lucky to stay on the pitch.

HACKED OFF WITH THE HAKA

Cockerill v Hewitt

Well, what did they expect? In 1997 at Old Trafford, New Zealand seriously seemed to think England's bolshy hooker Richard Cockerill would respect their pre-match Haka. No chance. Far from keeping a respectful distance, Cockerill marched forward until he stood eyeball to eyeball with his opposite number, Norm Hewitt. For several tense moments, it appeared that the Haka would end up as a punch-up. Fortunately, Hewitt and his All Black chums were able to restrain themselves in the face of this affront – and promptly got their own back by beating England.

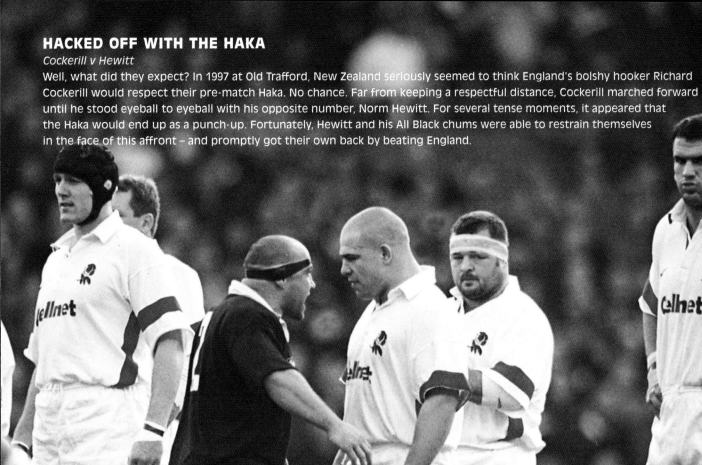

Ay oop, gis that t'fiver or ah'll smack thee!

John Bentley offers James Small his hand after the match, but Small rejects it

MOUTHY SPRINGBOK MEETS A LION UNCAGED

Small v Bentley

When the headcases of two hemispheres meet on the rugby pitch, a rumble is bound to occur. And so it came to pass that when James Small, renowned South African rabblerouser, came skinhead to skinhead with John Bentley during the 1997 Lions tour, there were fireworks. Small began winding Bentley up, which didn't please the Yorkshireman at all, and he slammed Small into touch, sparking a nose-to-nose confrontation. Bentley then scored twice past his opponent in a 38-21 win over Western Province.

Small was slaughtered by the South African press, and responded by alleging that Bentos had gouged his eye. Sadly for all handbag aficionados, an injury to Small prevented the simmering feud from erupting during the Test matches.

HI HO SILVA LINING, AND AWAY YOU GO...

Argentina v ACT

During the first match of Argentina's 1995 tour to Australia against ACT, a huge 30-man brawl broke out in the middle of the pitch. When the punch-up had finally subsided, the referee decided that punishment was required – and duly sent off Argentine centre Diego Cuesta-Silva (pictured), who was entitled to feel aggrieved as he had been nowhere near the action when it kicked off.

'WE WILL FIGHT THEM ON THE BEACHES...'

Skinner v Champ

It was a case of Mick the Munch versus Champ the Chump during the 1991 World Cup quarter-final in Paris. Champ, much-vaunted back row hero of France, was made to look like mincemeat by England's towering back three of Winterbottom, Teague and, above all, the rampaging Skinner who had one of his greatest games for England by consistently getting up the nose of Champ and his chums. Agincourt-style defiance by the big Geordie.

THE PRIDE OF LIONS

Hare v Canterbury

The British Lions of the 1983 tour to New Zealand might not have been much cop playing wise, but in a match against Canterbury, they proved their spurs in the martial arts. Canterbury hooker Hika Reid was the culprit this time, punching out at one of the Lions' front row. True to form, this was the signal for a huge all-out brawl featuring such luminaries as Scotland's Ian Paxton and Geoff Squire of Wales. Star performer, however, was England's Dusty Hare – a man not renowned for his fisticuffs – who raced into the thick of the action to deliver a punch, before legging it away as fast as possible.

Best of pals: Reid (left), Paxton and a wounded Dusty Hare

Colin Smart is overjoyed to see Nick Jeavons catch his wig

The RABBLE ROUSERS XV

TONY
O'REILLY

SERGE
BLANCO

JAMES
SMALL

WILL
CARLING

GEOFF
SHAW

STUART
BARNES

STEVE
SMITH

DEAN
RICHARDS

JOHN
JEFFREY

DEREK
WHITE

GORDON
BROWN

MAURICE
COLCLOUGH

MICK
GALWEY

RICHARD
COCKERILL

COLIN
SMART

E very team has its rabblerouser – the bloke who will drop his trousers at the drop of a hat, will gladly spray Ralgex on his own wedding tackle, be sick down the chairman's blazer, and who is the first to call for the yard of ale when the clubhouse is getting a bit quiet. Even at the very top end of the game there are rabblerousers. Indeed, some of their exploits are legendary simply because they were performed on the world stage. Here, then, are 15 players the old farts certainly wouldn't let anywhere near the members' bar.

Cool Hand Blanco and the French team ponder which type of performance to put on today

Serge in pimp moustache shock. 'Eez cool, huh?'

FULL BACK
SERGE BLANCO

Another call-up for the Frenchman, who played for years at the highest level despite a taste for wine and a 40-a-day cigarette habit. Indeed, Blanco claimed his lifestyle helped him. When one French coach forced the full back to give up fags, Blanco put on so much weight that he was allowed to start smoking again.

CENTRE
WILL CARLING

The former England skipper's devastating tackle and his eye for a pretty blonde earns him a place in our illustrious XV – although Carling's rabble-rousing was not restricted to the opposite sex. One of the prime movers of professionalism in British rugby, Carling enjoyed baiting the administrators almost as much as dating chicks. When he called the RFU committee "57 old farts", he was proved right when the aforementioned old farts banned him briefly from the England team. Carling rubbed many people up the wrong way, however, and it was perceived as justice when, after dumping girlfriend Ali Cockayne, the mother of his child, public opinion forced him to abandon a lucrative testimonial at Wembley.

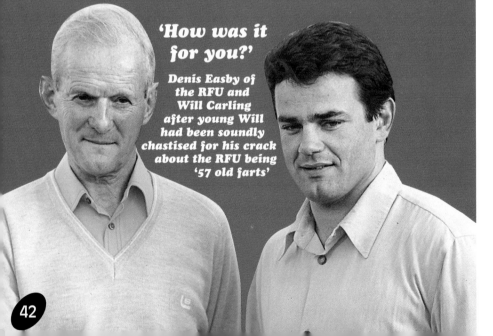

'How was it for you?'

Denis Easby of the RFU and Will Carling after young Will had been soundly chastised for his crack about the RFU being '57 old farts'

WING
JAMES SMALL
(Captain)

South African James Small has consistently proved that whatever feats he can perform on the pitch, it is off it where he is most in his element. Banned after being sent off for verbal abuse of the referee in Australia in 1993, Small got into further trouble with a pre-Test dust-up in a beach bar. Redeeming himself with a brave and effective performance against Jonah Lomu in the 1995 World Cup final, Small once again blotted his copybook a year later when he was caught boozing in a nightclub the night before a Tri-Nations match.

WING
TONY O'REILLY

After a successful playing career for Ireland and the Lions, Tony O'Reilly went on to become the multi-millionaire boss of Heinz and later a newspaper magnate. But even as a player, he enjoyed the high life, expressing a fervent dedication to the social side of the game. His finest

SECOND ROW
GORDON BROWN

'Broon Frae Troon' was an integral part of the Lions tours of 1971, '74 and '77 – not only as a player but, more importantly, on the social side where his alcohol consumption was matched only by his storytelling. Brown famously tells of one match in South Africa where his opposite number lost his glass eye in a ruck. Having courteously helped to find it, Brown was spooked when he later saw the same player standing at a line-out with the eye in place – and a large clump of grass poking from the socket.

match was probably his last for Ireland in 1970 against England. O'Reilly (right), who happened to be in London on business, was the last-minute emergency replacement for injured winger Bill Brown. Aged 34, overweight and nowhere near match fitness, he arrived at Twickenham in a chauffeur-driven Rolls-Royce. In the changing room, skipper Willie John McBride famously remarked, "Tony, you are no longer in your prime – the tactic I suggest you adopt is to shake your jowls at your opposite number!"

CENTRE
GEOFF SHAW

Weighing in at a whopping 16st, Geoff 'Bunter' Shaw was the original top Aussie bloke. Capped 28 times by Australia between 1969 and 1979 including nine times as skipper, Shaw preferred copious quantities of beer and barbies to any of that training nonsense. On the pitch, he was like a Sherman tank in the centre of the field. It has been said that he virtually invented the concept of deliberately taking out two tacklers in midfield to create more space for the rest of the team – assuming, that is, that anyone actually wanted to tackle him. However, those brave enough to make the attempt knew that Bunter would always get the beers in afterwards.

FLY HALF
STUART BARNES

In the great Barnes-v-Andrew debate, there is no doubt that of the two England fly halves you would prefer to be on the piss with Stuart Barnes. During a frustrating career in which Goldenbollocks consistently got the nod, the roly-poly man from Bath certainly had good reason to drown his sorrows with a few bottles of his beloved claret, beer, cider or whatever happened to be to hand. Pity, really, for on his day Barnesie (left) was a brilliant player with far more flair than the boot-oriented Andrew. The try he set up for Rory Underwood during the Calcutta Cup match against Scotland in 1993 is one that most rugby fans will drink to for ever and a day.

SCRUM HALF
STEVE SMITH

England's Steve Smith would readily admit that if it wasn't for his old mate Fran Cotton dragging him up hill and down dale, he would never have been fit enough to play rugby for England. Smithy (left) always preferred a few beers with the lads to an intensive training session. Hugely popular with team-mates and fans alike, he had a highly developed sense of humour – something that every England player during the dire 1970s and 1980s required.

PROP
COLIN SMART

Big Colin Smart was the man at the middle of perhaps the most famous rabble-rousing incident of all time. During a post-France v England dinner in Paris in 1982, Smart and Maurice Colclough engaged in a drinking duel. As his pièce de résistance, Colclough picked up a bottle of aftershave, given to each England player by the French, and downed it in one. Not to be outdone, Smart glugged down his bottle. Unfortunately for Smart, Colclough had secretly emptied his own bottle and refilled it with water. Smart eventually saw the funny side – but only after his stomach had been pumped at a Parisian hospital.

PROP
MICK GALWEY

On tour with the Lions to New Zealand in 1993, wild Irish prop Mick Galwey decided he'd have a whirl round the local go-kart track. A couple of hours later, having written off several cars, he was banned from every karting track in the country.

SECOND ROW
MAURICE COLCLOUGH

His post-match boozing was legendary, as Colin Smart would testify. But then again, when he was first selected by England, Maurice Colclough was still a student – with a student's appetite for alcohol. He also favoured student fashion. Bill Beaumont recalls Colclough turning up to England squad sessions looking like a character from Withnail And I, in a greatcoat that had seen better days and carrying his rugby kit in a plastic bag.

BACK ROW
JOHN JEFFREY, DEAN RICHARDS, DEREK WHITE

The 1988 Calcutta Cup match at Murrayfield was a dull affair which the Sassenachs won 9-6. The post-match dinner, however, more than made up for the stale fare on the pitch. In a top Edinburgh hotel, both teams sat through the arduous preliminaries and speeches before getting absolutely hammered. Putting aside any differences they might have had on the pitch, a number of players – led by the back-row trio of Scots John Jeffrey (right) and Derek White, and Dean Richards (left) of England – decided to continue the evening's revelry with a tour of the pubs down Princes Street. And to complete the party, they decided to take the Calcutta Cup with them. Some intricate, international-style interpassing of the old trophy followed until, in typical back row style, the Cup was dropped. Rather than pick it up, however, they fly-hacked the Cup – fashioned from silver rupees – for several yards down Princes Street, incurring thousands of pounds of damage and the new name of the Calcutta Plate. Officials from both sides did their utmost to track down the culprits, but eventually gave up and had a whip-round to repair the Cup to its former glory.

An artist's impression of the legendary Calcutta Cup 'incident'

'No I bloody won't kiss yer!'

British Lion John Bentley works up a head
of steam as he evades Gauteng hooker
James Dalton en route to his classic try

The
MOMENTS
OF GENIUS
XV

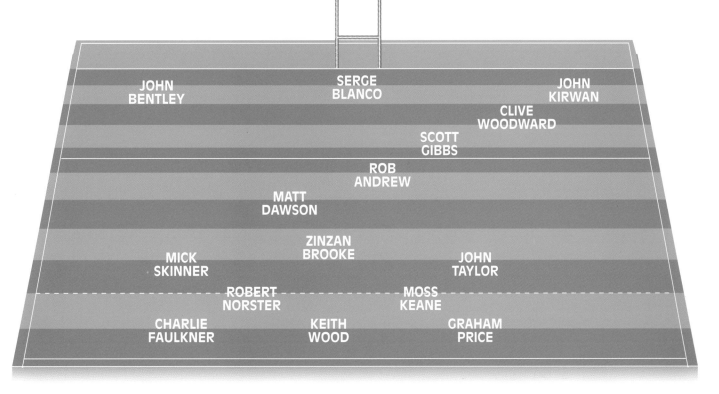

JOHN
BENTLEY

SERGE
BLANCO

JOHN
KIRWAN

CLIVE
WOODWARD

SCOTT
GIBBS

ROB
ANDREW

MATT
DAWSON

ZINZAN
BROOKE

MICK
SKINNER

JOHN
TAYLOR

ROBERT
NORSTER

MOSS
KEANE

CHARLIE
FAULKNER

KEITH
WOOD

GRAHAM
PRICE

Every so often a rugby match is transformed by a moment of genius. It might be a piece of sublime skill which leaves the opposition grasping at thin air, or a supreme physical effort which leads to a remarkable try. Either way, these moments are the essence of rugby – the moments which keep us coming back for more.

John Bentley touches down an unforgettable try which was a turning point in the Lions tour

FLY HALF
ROB ANDREW

THERE are seconds to go in a nailbiting World Cup '95 quarter-final between England and Australia in Cape Town. The scores are level at 22-22. England have a line-out in the Australian half. Bayfield catches and drives deep into green and gold territory, his fellow forwards straining behind him to make the maximum yardage. After what seems an eternity, scrum half Dewi Morris grabs the ball from the back of the maul and flings it back to Rob Andrew, standing ready some 40 metres out. Aussie fly half Michael Lynagh charges despairingly as Andrew, calm and collected, drops a prodigious goal which soars through the air and between the posts for an England win. They call Andrew "Goldenbollocks" – and that's why.

> "Martin Bayfield made a wonderful leap at the lineout. The forwards piled in behind, produced the ball – and all I could hope was that the kick would go over. It did, and suddenly there was pandemonium..."
>
> – ROB ANDREW
> *writing in World Cup: Rugby's Battle Of The Giants*

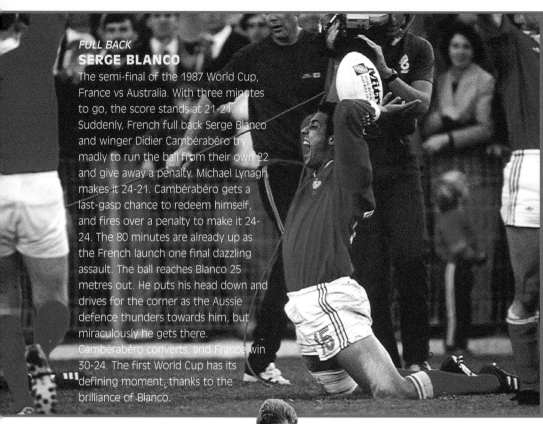

FULL BACK
SERGE BLANCO

The semi-final of the 1987 World Cup, France vs Australia. With three minutes to go, the score stands at 21-21. Suddenly, French full back Serge Blanco and winger Didier Cambérabéro try madly to run the ball from their own 22 and give away a penalty. Michael Lynagh makes it 24-21. Cambérabéro gets a last-gasp chance to redeem himself, and fires over a penalty to make it 24-24. The 80 minutes are already up as the French launch one final dazzling assault. The ball reaches Blanco 25 metres out. He puts his head down and drives for the corner as the Aussie defence thunders towards him, but miraculously he gets there. Cambérabéro converts, and France win 30-24. The first World Cup has its defining moment, thanks to the brilliance of Blanco.

"By now it was deep in injury time and we were waiting and waiting for the referee to blow for full-time. But play went on ... and on! And then came a sequence of play which was something else. There were so many of us involved – to me, to Lagisquet, to Rodriguez – we lost the ball, we got it back – and so the ball went back to me. What a moment for me! I was absolutely inspired by this great rolling wave of play to make a supreme effort. I threw myself over the line ... and that was it! Victory!"
– SERGE BLANCO
in the book World Cup: Rugby's Battle Of The Giants (Generation Publications)

WING
JOHN KIRWAN

The first match of the inaugural World Cup of 1987, and New Zealand were in no mood to play generous hosts. Lambs to the slaughter that day at Eden Park, Auckland, were the hapless Italians – they were thrashed 70-6. Amid the flurry of tries was an absolute gem from powerful winger John Kirwan. Receiving the ball virtually on his own try line, Kirwan set off on a rampage. He ran rings round the entire Italian team, sidestepping and selling dummies as if they were going out of fashion, leaving half a dozen tacklers sprawled on the ground, before bursting clear at the other end of the field to score unmolested between the posts. Indeed such was Kirwan's mood, he could have probably turned round and run through the woeful Italian defence again.

WING
JOHN BENTLEY

An unexpected call-up to the Lions squad to South Africa in 1997, England's John Bentley nevertheless went on to enjoy a highly successful tour, pitting his rugby league-honed power against the tough guys from the veld. And, during a midweek game against Gauteng, 'Bentos' scored the try of the tour. There seemed to be little on when the foursquare Yorkshireman received the ball wide on the right, just outside his own 22. But, showing tremendous pace and power, he set off on a mazy, sidestepping run that took him on an arcing path towards the posts and left the Gauteng defence clutching at thin air. With two defenders clinging on for dear life, Bentley bulldozed his way to the line and crashed over for a sensational try, clinching a narrow 20-14 victory.

CENTRE
CLIVE WOODWARD

How England these days could do with a centre of such elusive running ability as their coach Clive Woodward in his heyday (inset). During a hard-fought 23-17 win over Scotland in 1981, England won a line-out inside the Scottish half. In typically ponderous fashion, the ball finally reached Woodward on the Scots' 10-metre line. Seeing that there was nothing else on, Woodward set off on a mazy, mesmerising run through the heart of the blue-shirted defence, emerging several side-steps later just five yards from the line in order to plunge over for the try of the season.

SCRUM HALF
MATT DAWSON

Robert Howley's unfortunate injury early in the Lions tour of South Africa deprived the tourists of not only their number one scrum half, but one of their top players. Or so the thinking went. Replacement Matt Dawson had other ideas, and set about making headlines of his own during the crunch Test matches.

With seven minutes to go in the First Test in Cape Town, the Lions were trailing 16-15 but had a scrum just inside the Boks' 22. Dawson picked up and darted blind then dummied a one-handed pass inside which suckered three defenders. With the route to the line clear, the Northampton man strolled over for a decisive try (pictured below). The Lions went on to win the game 25-16.

Dawson won the first Test with a brilliant try (left)

CENTRE
SCOTT GIBBS

Known more for his crunching tackles than his twinkle toes, Gibbs danced through England's defence to spur a famous Welsh victory in the 1999 Five Nations match at Wembley. From a disputed penalty in the dying seconds, Wales won a line-out on the England 22. Chris Wyatt tapped it to Scott Quinnell, who fed Gibbs in midfield. The barrel-chested centre broke the first tackle then weaved through three more before leaving full back Matt Perry flat-footed and diving over to score. Jenkins added the conversion and Wales had won an extraordinary game 32-31. Cue wild scenes of joy…

PROP
CHARLIE FAULKNER

One third of the infamous Viet Gwent front row with Graham Price and Bobby Windsor, Charlie Faulkner found himself in the unaccustomed role of try scorer in a 30-point Five Nations thrashing dished out to Ireland in 1975. Ironically, considering the superlative Welsh backs of the time, it was a score set up by the forwards – and hooker Windsor in particular. After his burst down the left wing, Windsor popped it inside to Faulkner 20 yards out. With the cheekiest of side-steps, the Pontypool prop ghosted past two defenders and bulldozed his way to the line to the delight of the Cardiff crowd.

PROP
GRAHAM PRICE

A few weeks later, it was a case of anything you can do, I can do better. With Wales winning but on the rack at muddy Parc des Princes, salvation came in a most unexpected form. A clearance from Gareth Edwards was charged down deep in the Welsh 22 but the ball bounced to Graham Price, who wellied it 70 yards downfield. The French full back seemed to have it covered, but from nowhere winger J J Williams appeared to tackle him. Unbelievably, the ball squirted up straight into the hands of the supporting Price – who simply fell over the line to score. Final score: France 10 Wales 25.

HOOKER
KEITH WOOD

Ireland slumped out of the 1999 World Cup largely because of their lack of tries. And when they did manage to cross the

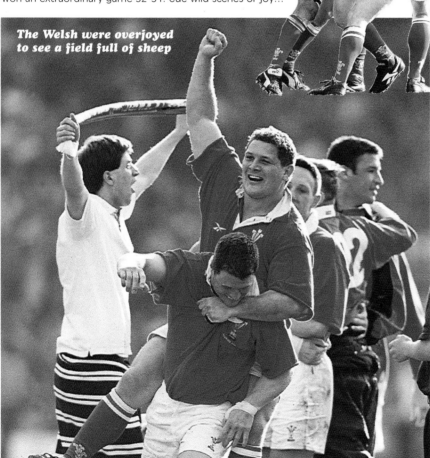

The Welsh were overjoyed to see a field full of sheep

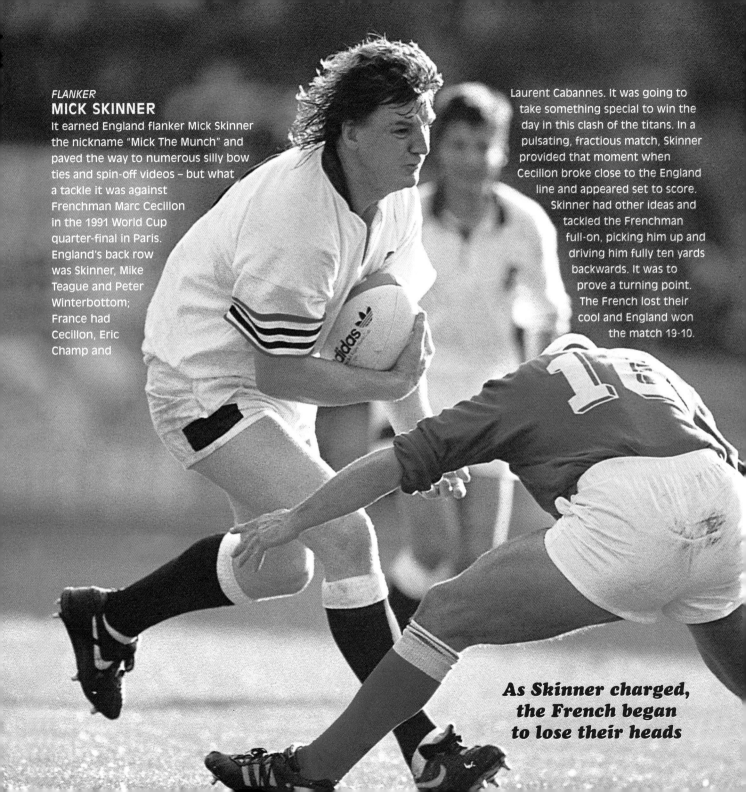

FLANKER
MICK SKINNER

It earned England flanker Mick Skinner the nickname "Mick The Munch" and paved the way to numerous silly bow ties and spin-off videos – but what a tackle it was against Frenchman Marc Cecillon in the 1991 World Cup quarter-final in Paris. England's back row was Skinner, Mike Teague and Peter Winterbottom; France had Cecillon, Eric Champ and Laurent Cabannes. It was going to take something special to win the day in this clash of the titans. In a pulsating, fractious match, Skinner provided that moment when Cecillon broke close to the England line and appeared set to score. Skinner had other ideas and tackled the Frenchman full-on, picking him up and driving him fully ten yards backwards. It was to prove a turning point. The French lost their cool and England won the match 19-10.

As Skinner charged, the French began to lose their heads

Zinzan Brooke scores a great drop goal despite the English defence trying to pull his shorts down

line, it was not a back but a hooker who scored 'em. The 53-8 thrashing of the USA at Lansdowne Road was a personal triumph for the irrepressible Keith Wood. Out of the seven Irish tries scored, the skinheaded hooker notched up four in an extraordinary solo performance which matched Brian Robinson's 1991 record for the most tries by an Irishman in a Test.

SECOND ROW
MOSS KEANE

That fag-smoking, Guinness-swilling Moss Keane should be anywhere near the try-line was unusual enough. The fact that he put a skilful finishing touch to a scintillating Irish try during their 22-15 win over Scotland in Dublin in 1980 was almost unbelievable. Keane began the try by tapping a short line-out to scrum half Colin Patterson. Patterson fed Ollie Campbell, who scythed through the Scottish defence to the 22. When he was stopped, the ball was flipped across to the usually lumbering Keane, who showed an amazing turn of pace to outstrip Andy Irvine and score near the posts.

SECOND ROW
ROBERT NORSTER

A great line-out jumper, Wales lock Bob Norster showed blistering pace to score against Ireland at Cardiff in 1987. Architect of the score was fly half Jonathan Davies, who made a few yards in the loose. A neat reverse pass and suddenly, from nowhere, Norster was charging through to score from 20 yards with what remained of the Irish defence clinging to his back. A moment of triumph for Norster, but not for Wales who lost 15-11.

FLANKER
JOHN TAYLOR

Now known as a commentator, John Taylor was a highly effective flanker for Wales and the Lions, despite looking like a frazzled garden gnome. He was also no mean goalkicker in the days when the ball was like a soggy pudding when wet. Just such a scenario greeted Taylor at Murrayfield in 1971. A last-minute Gerald Davies try had brought Wales to within one point of Scotland. The Welsh team couldn't bear to watch the conversion attempt; but from out on the right touchline, and with the lights of Edinburgh twinkling in the gloaming, Taylor nervelessly toe-ended it between the sticks to earn a 19-18 victory. Wales duly went on to win the Grand Slam.

No. 8
ZINZAN BROOKE *(Captain)*

If ever there was a case of adding insult to injury, Zinzan Brooke's outrageous drop goal in the 1995 World Cup semi-final against England takes the biscuit. Already stunned after Jonah Lomu and Josh Kronfeld had scored tries in the first five minutes, bewildered England then watched as Will Carling's desperate clearing punt was caught on halfway by the New Zealand No. 8. Brooke promptly launched a drop kick from 50 metres out which flew sweetly between the sticks. As Gerald Davies wrote in World Cup: Rugby's Battle Of The Giants: "This was so audacious, the crowd looked on open-mouthed, hardly believing what they were seeing."

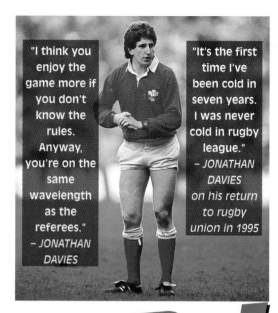

"I think you enjoy the game more if you don't know the rules. Anyway, you're on the same wavelength as the referees."
– JONATHAN DAVIES

"It's the first time I've been cold in seven years. I was never cold in rugby league."
– JONATHAN DAVIES on his return to rugby union in 1995

"I'm 49, I've had a brain haemorrhage and a triple bypass, and I could still go out and play a reasonable game of rugby union. But I wouldn't last 30 seconds in rugby league."
– GRAHAM LOWE, former coach of Wigan

"Gareth Edwards? The sooner that little so-and-so goes to rugby league, the better it will be for all of us."
– DICKIE JEEPS of England, 1967

DID I REALLY

"To me rugby is an opportunity to show how creative you can be and I know what can be done if you decide to have a go. I can accept losing if you've at least had a go. But to lose and be boring in the process is something that can only be detrimental to rugby. Those who can't break the defence by running the ball or setting up their back line should not be on the field."
– DAVID CAMPESE

Campese's goosestep made his legs as wide as his mouth

"The only thing you're ever likely to get on the end of an English back line is chilblains."
– DAVID CAMPESE

"A sharp dresser who likes to show his biceps off in tight-fitting T-shirts that are a couple of sizes too small for him."
– JOHN BENTLEY on Neil Back (right), in his book Lions Uncaged

"You know exactly what he is going to do. He's going to come off his right foot at great speed. You also know that there isn't a blind thing you can do about it."
– DAVID DUCKHAM, England winger, on Welsh genius Gerald Davies

"You'd need a fork lift truck to lift him in the lineout."
– BILL BEAUMONT on France lock Olivier Merle

"The fastest prop in the game."
– *JEREMY GUSCOTT on Scott Gibbs*

SAY THAT??

A typical day at the office

"No leadership, no ideas. Not even enough imagination to thump someone in the lineout when the ref wasn't looking."
– *JPR WILLIAMS after a Welsh defeat*

"Dean Richards is nicknamed Warren, as in 'warren ugly bastard'."
– *JASON LEONARD*

"The backs preen themselves and the forwards drink."
DEAN RICHARDS reveals what goes on after the game

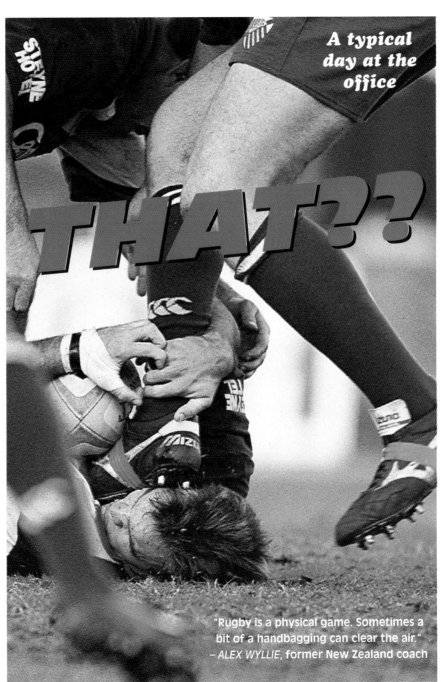

"Rugby is a physical game. Sometimes a bit of a handbagging can clear the air."
– *ALEX WYLLIE*, **former New Zealand coach**

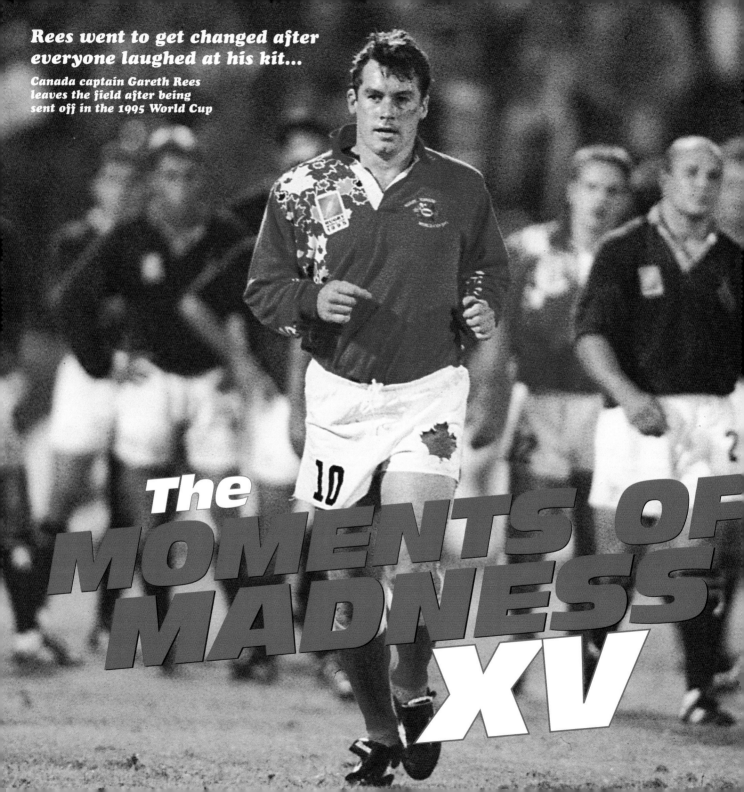

Rees went to get changed after everyone laughed at his kit...

Canada captain Gareth Rees leaves the field after being sent off in the 1995 World Cup

The MOMENTS OF MADNESS XV

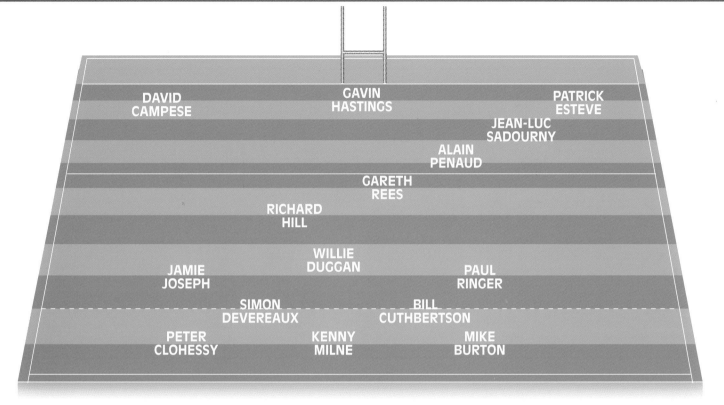

DAVID
CAMPESE

GAVIN
HASTINGS

PATRICK
ESTEVE

JEAN-LUC
SADOURNY

ALAIN
PENAUD

GARETH
REES

RICHARD
HILL

WILLIE
DUGGAN

JAMIE
JOSEPH

PAUL
RINGER

SIMON
DEVEREAUX

BILL
CUTHBERTSON

PETER
CLOHESSY

KENNY
MILNE

MIKE
BURTON

Just as moments of rugby genius are there to be savoured for years to come, so moments of madness are part and parcel of this great game's rich folklore. Whether it's an inexplicable fumble by the greatest player in the world as he is about to cross the try-line, or a right hook swung through the red mist that costs a team victory, these are moments to celebrate – and just thank Christ it wasn't you.

Good looks run in the family: Kenny Milne with brothers Iain and David

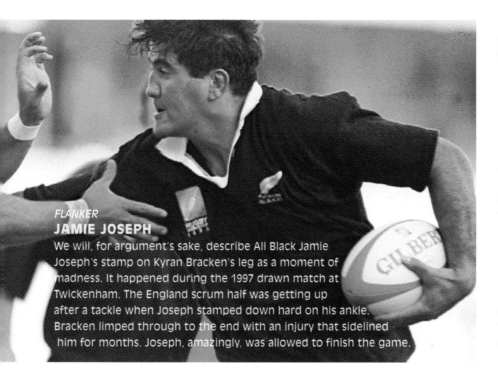

FLANKER
JAMIE JOSEPH

We will, for argument's sake, describe All Black Jamie Joseph's stamp on Kyran Bracken's leg as a moment of madness. It happened during the 1997 drawn match at Twickenham. The England scrum half was getting up after a tackle when Joseph stamped down hard on his ankle. Bracken limped through to the end with an injury that sidelined him for months. Joseph, amazingly, was allowed to finish the game.

WING
DAVID CAMPESE

It takes a lot to silence Australian winger David Campese. But on this occasion – the crucial Third Test between the Wallabies and the Lions in 1989 – it was Campo's own foot that was in his mouth.

It was a howler to relish. With the scores evenly poised, Campese fielded the ball on his own goal line. Instead of booting it away, however, he flung a hopelessly speculative pass to full back Greg Martin. The ball bounced loose and Lions winger Ieuan Evans pounced gleefully upon it to score a try.

The score turned the match the tourists' way, and they went on to conclude a historic series win. Typically, Campo's attitude afterwards was "You win

some, you lose some". But former Wallaby skipper Andy Slack commented: "You do not play Mickey Mouse rugby in the green and gold of Australia. He's part of a team and if he can't act that way, he's better off playing tennis."

WING
PATRICK ESTEVE

Nicknamed the Bayonne Express, grey-faced French winger Patrick Estève looked more like the Bayonne Corpse. And he must have wished he was six feet under after his monumental clanger in the 1985 match against England.

Having steamed past the defence and over the England line for a try, Estève decided to race just a few more yards nearer the posts to make the conversion easier. Unfortunately, the opposition scrum half Nigel Melville was on hand to knock the ball out of Estève's hands. The match ended a 9-9 draw.

CENTRES
JEAN-LUC SADOURNY
ALAIN PENAUD

According to their passports, Alain Penaud is a fly half and Jean-Luc Sadourny is a full back. But such are the vagaries of French selection, both have played in most other positions in the back line. With such confusion, a cock-up was bound to occur sooner or later – and when it did, it was a classic. Against England in 1992, France won possession inside their own half and the ball was whipped along the threequarters. Sadourny and Penaud attempted an intricate scissors move in the middle of the park, the kind that normally ends up in a magnificent try for les Bleus. On this occasion, however, the try was England's as the two Frenchmen ran into each other and the ball ballooned into the hands of a delighted English team, who ran on to score.

Patrick Estève tries not to drop the ball – or bump into any team-mates

FLY HALF
GARETH REES

Canadian fat boy Gareth Rees is the proud holder of the record of having played in all four World Cups. But in 1995, he became a member of an equally exclusive club – fly halves who have been sent off. It happened during an explosive tie against hosts South Africa. Seeing full back Scott Stewart being roughed up during one of the game's many fights, Rees got stuck in with a couple of haymakers of his own. The referee promptly sent him for an early bath.

PROP
MIKE BURTON

It was always going to take something special to become the first England player to be sent off, and prop Mike Burton's big moment against Australia in 1975's Battle of Ballymore was just that. A

SCRUM HALF
RICHARD HILL

It was a proud moment for Bath scrum half Richard Hill: captain of England at last, with a good chance of winning at Cardiff for the first time in 24 years. Within seconds of this 1987 Five Nations match, however, it all went pear- shaped. From the kick-off Hill, along with Wade Dooley, Gareth Chilcott and Graham Dawe, got into a mass brawl with the Welsh pack. England lost 19-12 and Hill and his fellow scrappers were suspended by the RFU.

"I'm handbags at dawn at the best of times, but when I saw Scott Stewart being held by two South Africans and punched by a third, I reacted. I thought referee McHugh was calling me over as captain, so when he told me I was sent off, I was absolutely shocked. My mum says it was character-building!"
GARETH REES, pictured with fellow early bather Rod Snow

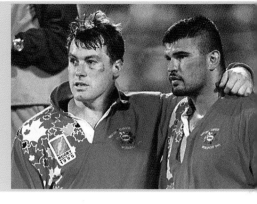

volatile match exploded in spectacular style with two massive brawls. Soon after, Aussie wing Dave Osborne launched an up-and-under – and was watching the ball land when he was felled with a straight arm smash by the horrendously late Burton.

HOOKER
KENNY MILNE

Scotland's Kenny Milne was a feisty competitor who gave as good as he got. While playing for Heriot's against Jed-Forest, Milne decided to settle a score with his opposing hooker. As the front rows lined up, Milne threw a punch – but missed his target and flattened the referee instead. Ban ahoy!

SECOND ROW
BILL CUTHBERTSON

It was during Scotland's tour of Australia in 1982 that Bill Cuthbertson had a moment of madness which

nearly cost him his life. During a day off at Surfer's Paradise, he decided to go for a swim – despite dire warnings about the current. It took three of his colleagues to pull the half-drowned lock from the water.

SECOND ROW
SIMON DEVEREAUX

Gloucester's Simon Devereaux had plenty of time to reflect on his moment of madness – four months, to be precise. That's how long he spent in Wandsworth prison after punching Rosslyn Park's Jamie Cowie during a match in 1995. Cowie's jaw was broken in three places and Devereaux was convicted of GBH.

FLANKER
PAUL RINGER

The sending-off of Wales flanker Paul Ringer after 15 minutes of the crunch Five Nations clash at Twickenham in 1980 was inevitable. For days before, the press had whipped up a frenzy. Ringer provided the moment of madness with a late tackle on England fly half John Horton. It wasn't the worst late tackle ever seen. But it was possibly the most stupid. England won 9-8 and went on to the Grand Slam.

'Och, this one'll be nae bother...'

Gavin Hastings lines up the easy penalty kick that will haunt him for years

No. 8
WILLIE DUGGAN

It is difficult to pinpoint a single moment of madness for Willie Duggan – the Irish No.8's career seemed to be one long moment of madness. Perhaps the pivotal moment for the 'Blackrock Bomber' came in 1977 when, during a game against Wales, Duggan reached across and thumped Geoff Wheel for no reason whatsoever. Wheel quickly recovered his senses and belted Duggan back. The pair continued slugging it out, unaware that the referee was standing beside them. Neither had any complaints as they became the first players ever to be sent off in the Five Nations.

PROP
PETER CLOHESSY

Irish prop Peter Clohessy must have thought he'd got away with stamping on Olivier Roumat's head during a Five Nations clash with France in 1996. However, Clohessy's moment of madness was captured perfectly by a cameraman at Parc des Princes. The subsequent footage earned the Irishman a six-month ban.

FULL BACK
GAVIN HASTINGS

The 1991 World Cup semi-final between England and Scotland had been a dismal affair, largely thanks to England's negative tactics. So when Scotland were awarded a penalty with the score at 6-6 and time running out, Gavin Hastings had the chance to give the home side a potentially match-winning lead and put the game out of its misery. Barely 30 yards out and directly in front of the sticks, you would have bet your kilt on the unerring Scottish full back drilling it home. Yet, inexplicably, the big man pushed it wide of the posts. A moment of madness indeed – and one which cost his side dear. With barely minutes remaining, old Goldenbollocks Rob Andrew sealed a narrow England win with a trademark drop goal.

Leprechaun on the rampage!

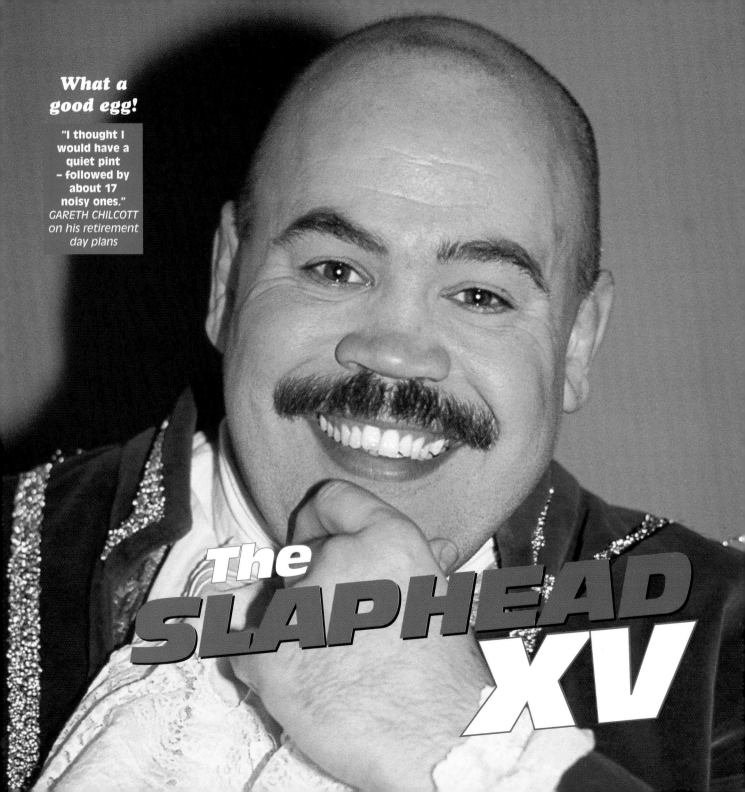

What a good egg!

"I thought I would have a quiet pint – followed by about 17 noisy ones."
GARETH CHILCOTT on his retirement day plans

The SLAPHEAD XV

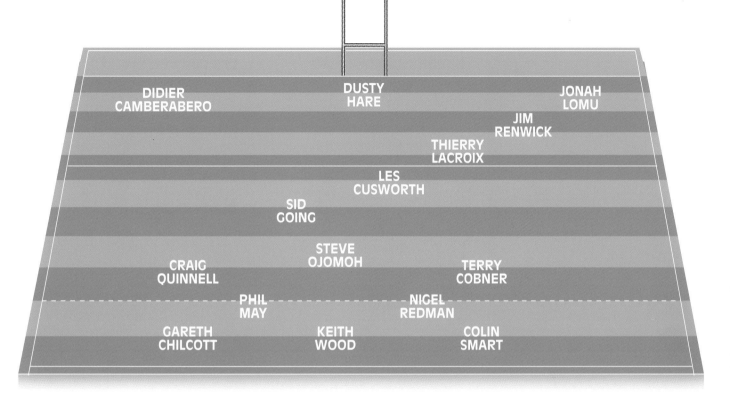

DIDIER
CAMBERABERO

DUSTY
HARE

JONAH
LOMU

JIM
RENWICK

THIERRY
LACROIX

LES
CUSWORTH

SID
GOING

STEVE
OJOMOH

CRAIG
QUINNELL

TERRY
COBNER

PHIL
MAY

NIGEL
REDMAN

GARETH
CHILCOTT

KEITH
WOOD

COLIN
SMART

Before the 1995 World Cup, the entire French team shaved off their hair. And why not? After all, some of the rugby greats have been slapheads – towering talents whose prowess with the ball is surpassed only by their skill with the comb-over. Here, we pay homage to 15 of the best baldies to ever grace the game.

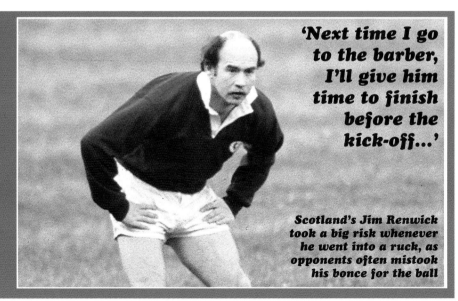

'Next time I go to the barber, I'll give him time to finish before the kick-off...'

Scotland's Jim Renwick took a big risk whenever he went into a ruck, as opponents often mistook his bonce for the ball

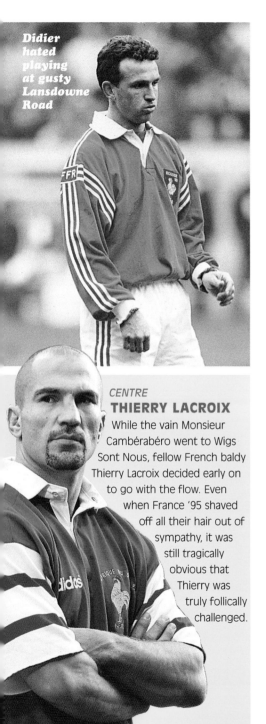

Didier hated playing at gusty Lansdowne Road

WING
DIDIER CAMBERABERO

"Quoi??" you might think, looking at pictures of the great French utility back, "but Didier Cambérabéro has got a beautiful head of luxuriant locks!" Indeed he has – but so has William Shatner. Yes, beneath that bouffant barnet, Didier is as bald as a coot. There's not many players who would risk wearing a syrup in such a rough-and-tumble sport as rugby – which says a great deal both for Cambérabéro's jinking abilities and for his preferred brand of glue.

CENTRE
JIM RENWICK

One of Scotland's finest centres, a player with pace and verve, Jim Renwick nevertheless always looked like one of the players' grandads on account of his amusing comb-over baldy hairstyle and moustache.

FLY HALF
LES CUSWORTH

The undisputed master of the 'pedal-bin' hairstyle, England's Les Cusworth ruled supreme during the early 1980s. A wily competitor, he often put opposing back rows to the sword by going one way while his hair went the other.

FULL BACK
DUSTY HARE

Christened William Henry Hare, the goalkicking Leicester and England legend was nicknamed 'Dusty'. However by the end of his distinguished career, 'Got No' would have been a more appropriate moniker.

CENTRE
THIERRY LACROIX

While the vain Monsieur Cambérabéro went to Wigs Sont Nous, fellow French baldy Thierry Lacroix decided early on to go with the flow. Even when France '95 shaved off all their hair out of sympathy, it was still tragically obvious that Thierry was truly follically challenged.

No one dared tell Jonah he looked bloody stupid

WING
JONAH LOMU

Admittedly his chrome-dome is self-inflicted, but Lomu merits a place in our Baldies XV for the simple reason that baldness – and the resulting lack of wind resistance – is now a recognised asset to top players in this professional era.

Can you pick out the boiled egg in this identity parade?

Les Cusworth:
The Full Moon

Nigel Redman:
The Millennium Dome

All Black baldy Jimmy Duncan used to play in a tweed cap to cover his pate, and once sold the Auckland defence a dummy by throwing his cap to the man outside him. The wrong-footed defence fell for it, and the bare-headed Duncan ran in for a try.

Keith Wood:
The Irish Mullet

Steve Ojomoh:
The Polished Finish

SCRUM HALF
SID GOING

Like Jim Renwick, New Zealand legend Sid Going always looked 50, even in his twenties. In the Land of the Long White Cloud, Going was a passionate advocate of the Long Strand of Hair Combed Over the Skull. Having said that, he was completely nails and very few opponents ever ruffled his delicate coiffure.

PROP
GARETH CHILCOTT

'Coochie' Chilcott, who performed sterling service for Bath and England, was going bald long before he decided to shave off all his hair. Unwittingly, he began a trend for skinhead front-rowers which has spread like wildfire in today's game.

PROP
COLIN SMART

Look at any third or fourth XV fixture today and you will see prop forwards who look like Colin Smart. Yet in the late 1970s, Smart – fat and bald – was the blueprint for your international front row forward. He enjoyed his pies, his beer and his aftershave (more of which elsewhere).

HOOKER
KEITH WOOD

These days it is quite unusual to find a hooker who actually has not shaved his hair off. So top marks to Keith Wood of Ireland – a genuine slaphead.

SECOND ROW
NIGEL REDMAN

While the England powerhouse of Wade Dooley and Paul Ackford gradually lost their hair match by match, their replacement Nigel Redman was a complete baldy on his international debut.

SECOND ROW
PHIL MAY

The Welsh lock is perhaps one of the reasons subsequent baldy forwards have gone for the whole hog No.1. A fine player, May's hard image was undermined by the fact that he looked like a monk.

FLANKER
TERRY COBNER

(Captain)

Another student of the comb-it-over school, Wales and British Lions dynamo Terry Cobner at least had the excuse that he was playing in the mid-Seventies when that sort of hairdo was all the rage among chrome-dome rugby players.

FLANKER
CRAIG QUINNELL

Balding Welsh flanker Craig Quinnell is one of the only players to have requested a Duncan Goodhew from his barber – a haircut so short that not even stubble remains.

NO.8
STEVE OJOMOH

Bald head glittering in the sunlight, there were few finer sights than Steve Ojomoh in full flight. Unfortunately, the decision to grow his hair again swiftly resulted in the England back row man becoming an ex-England back row man.

Seeing that his team-mates were ignoring him, Campo tried to make friends with the goalpost

The POSEURS XV

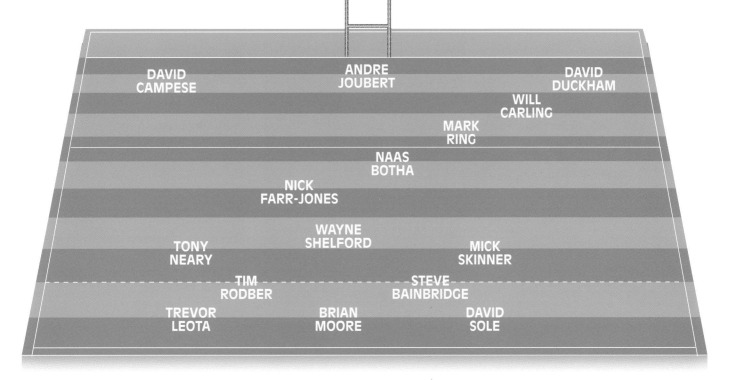

DAVID CAMPESE

ANDRE JOUBERT

DAVID DUCKHAM

WILL CARLING

MARK RING

NAAS BOTHA

NICK FARR-JONES

WAYNE SHELFORD

TONY NEARY

MICK SKINNER

TIM RODBER

STEVE BAINBRIDGE

TREVOR LEOTA

BRIAN MOORE

DAVID SOLE

There are two kinds of great rugby player: the modest type, who cares little for public adoration; and the poseur, for whom nothing less than a trumpet fanfare to herald his genius will suffice. This XV celebrates the latter – those players whose very demeanour suggests that they believe they inhabit a different rugby stratosphere to mere mortals … even if most mortals think they are complete tossers.

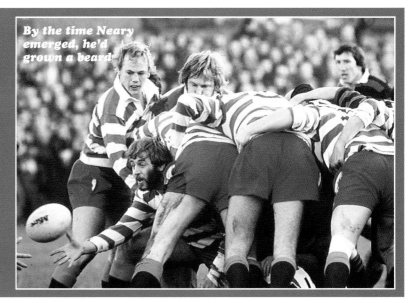

By the time Neary emerged, he'd grown a beard

69

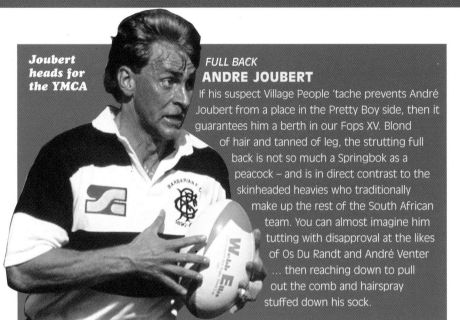

Joubert heads for the YMCA

FULL BACK
ANDRE JOUBERT

If his suspect Village People 'tache prevents André Joubert from a place in the Pretty Boy side, then it guarantees him a berth in our Fops XV. Blond of hair and tanned of leg, the strutting full back is not so much a Springbok as a peacock – and is in direct contrast to the skinheaded heavies who traditionally make up the rest of the South African team. You can almost imagine him tutting with disapproval at the likes of Os Du Randt and André Venter … then reaching down to pull out the comb and hairspray stuffed down his sock.

Botha posed patiently for the statue he had ordered

FLY HALF
NAAS BOTHA

In a position traditionally occupied by strutting show-offs, South African legend Naas Botha gets the nod for his over-powering belief in his own right boot. Botha knew he was the world's greatest kicker. The purpose of the other 14 players was to chase his kicks and retrieve the ball so that he could kick it again. A typical Botha performance came in the 1987 Currie Cup Final, which he won singlehandedly with four penalties and four drop goals. Though he was a proven matchwinner, opinion was divided between those who thought Botha was a genius and those who thought he was a selfish b*****d. Naas himself was in no doubt.

Without his specs, Nick never realised he was passing to nobody

SCRUM HALF
NICK FARR-JONES

Talented, good-looking, bespectacled, educated, bilingual, World Cup winner – Terry Holmes he ain't.

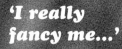

'I really fancy me...'

Will Carling at work, rest and play – and, amazingly, not a woman in sight

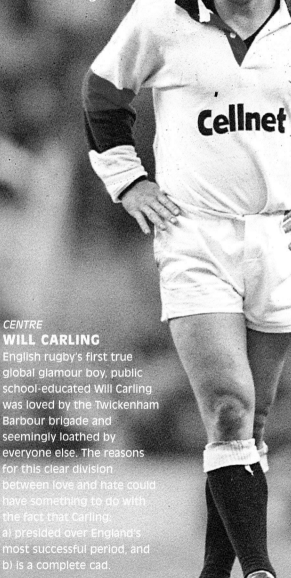

CENTRE
WILL CARLING
English rugby's first true global glamour boy, public school-educated Will Carling was loved by the Twickenham Barbour brigade and seemingly loathed by everyone else. The reasons for this clear division between love and hate could have something to do with the fact that Carling.
a) presided over England's most successful period, and
b) is a complete cad.

'Everyone knows there is a loose wire between Campo's brain and his mouth.'
BOB DWYER

WING
DAVID DUCKHAM

As England's best player by a street, flying winger David Duckham had every right to be aloof. Unfortunately, Duckham's international career coincided with England's dismal sides of the 1970s – which meant that between 1969 and 1976 he received only three passes. Admittedly he scored each time. Duckham in full flow was a sight to behold, his long legs striding out and his blond hair streaming behind him like a comet. He was a Twickenham hero – but it didn't stop the Coventry man wishing he'd been born Welsh.

Campo was a law unto himself. He knew he was a class above the rest – and didn't mind saying so. His team-mates were just an obstacle to his genius. "My first responsibility is to myself," Campo once said. "I want to satisfy myself by going out there and doing something you know no player in the world has ever managed to pull off." A top-class poseur – but Campo invariably succeeded in his aim.

PROP
DAVID SOLE

Quietly spoken and highly educated? Surely not the credentials of a player who slaves away at rugby's coal face. But Scotland's David Sole always had to be different. Once, he declined to attend a disciplinary hearing because he had to baby-sit. Under Sole's captaincy, Scotland ditched the National Anthem for Flower Of Scotland and marched on to the pitch rather than running like everyone else. He also led the jocks to victory over England and the 1990 Grand Slam – one of the biggest upsets in Five Nations history. And this was a bloke who not only played and lived in England but spoke with an English accent!

Why is a hooker like a solicitor? Because they both solicit...

HOOKER
BRIAN MOORE

Brian Moore always did have an eye for self-promotion. A few years ago, when he was still playing, it was impossible to find an advertising billboard that did not feature the England hooker's ugly mug staring out from it. Boots, cars, burgers, Pampers – it seemed there was nothing that 'Pitbull' would not put his name to. You'd have expected retirement to curtail his activities – but no, Pitbull still has a nice sideline in videos, and is now planning a career in politics. Worst of all, he has adopted a skinhead/goatee combo. What a poseur!

PROP
TREVOR LEOTA

Usually a hooker, Samoan Trevor Leota cannot be excluded from our Poseurs XV and so switches to prop. He gets the call on account of his dyed peroxide hair, which, when he first appeared for Wasps, set all the tongues wagging. But while his yellow-and-black mane helped Leota stand out from the crowd, it also drew attention to the fact that – typically hard Samoan tackling aside – he wasn't actually that good a player.

SECOND ROW
STEVE BAINBRIDGE

If a fight broke out during an England match in the 1980s, chances were it was started by second row Steve 'This one is for the ladies' Bainbridge. He certainly looked the part – rugged good looks, waxed legs, Bee Gees hairstyle – and when he put his mind to it he was a fine player. Trouble was, he couldn't fight his way out of a paper bag. His ineffectual flaps served only to annoy genuine hard men like Robert Norster, Alan Tomes and Moss Keane, resulting in mass brawls from which Bainbridge was mysteriously missing.

FLANKER
TONY NEARY

Like all the top rugby poseurs, Tony Neary's arrogance was based on the fact that he was a brilliant player both for England and the British Lions. But off the pitch, he raised two fingers to the rugby establishment at every opportunity – and ended up behind bars when he was convicted of stealing from a trust fund.

SECOND ROW
TIM RODBER

Tim Rodber: army man, iron hard second row, heart of oak, the type of stout yeoman that would lay his life down for his country.
Tim Rodber: poses for poncey pictures with his cuddly mutts. Say no more.

Come to Rodber country...

Macho man and country squire Tim shows off his modelling prowess

No. 8

WAYNE SHELFORD

He was an All Black legend and he knew it. But 'Buck' Shelford gets the nod at No. 8 in the Poseurs XV largely on the strength of the huge temper tantrum he threw after being dropped by New Zealand in 1990. Rather than fight his way back into the team, Shelford instead took his bat and ball and moved to England to coach Northampton. Poseurish behaviour indeed, but perhaps Shelford was right to be aggrieved about his treatment. After all, he gave his all for the All Blacks – including his right testicle, ripped from his scrotum during the 1986 defeat by France.

Shelford found the Haka a bit of a pain after the '86 game against France

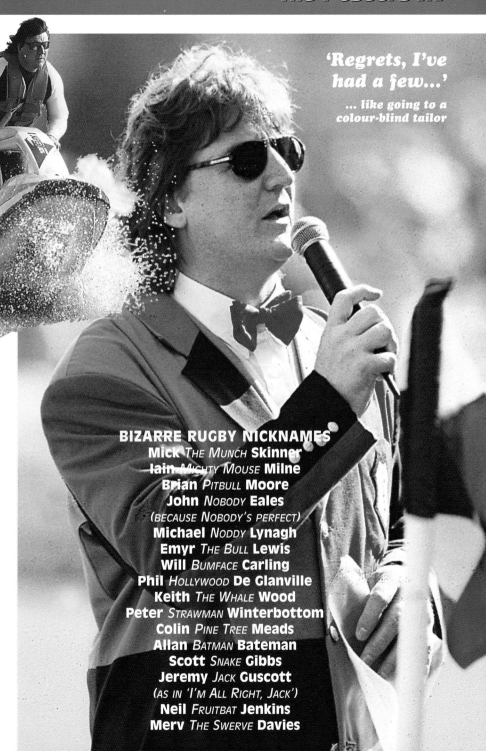

FLANKER
MICK SKINNER

In his new career as rugby's favourite wacky television pundit, former England flanker Mick 'The Munch' Skinner these days opts to wear Union Jack waistcoats and bow-ties fashioned from five-pound notes. There is a thin line between poseur and pillock but, largely because of his tackle on Marc Cecillon in 1991, we are prepared to give "The Munch" the benefit of the doubt.

CENTRE
MARK RING

You had to feel sorry for Mark Ring. There he was, probably the most talented centre in the world, playing amid the donkeys of 1980s Wales. If only he'd been born 10 years earlier, we might have mentioned him in the same breath as JPR, Gerald and Barry rather than Adrian Hadley, Mike Rayer and Emyr Lewis. Still, Ring made no bones about the fact he was Wales' best player, often trying outrageous things simply to relieve the boredom of watching Paul Thorburn kicking for goal. A poseur without a doubt, but an entertainer too.

'Regrets, I've had a few...'
... like going to a colour-blind tailor

BIZARRE RUGBY NICKNAMES
Mick *THE MUNCH* Skinner
Iain *MIGHTY MOUSE* Milne
Brian *PITBULL* Moore
John *NOBODY* Eales
(BECAUSE NOBODY'S PERFECT)
Michael *NODDY* Lynagh
Emyr *THE BULL* Lewis
Will *BUMFACE* Carling
Phil *HOLLYWOOD* De Glanville
Keith *THE WHALE* Wood
Peter *STRAWMAN* Winterbottom
Colin *PINE TREE* Meads
Allan *BATMAN* Bateman
Scott *SNAKE* Gibbs
Jeremy *JACK* Guscott
(AS IN 'I'M ALL RIGHT, JACK')
Neil *FRUITBAT* Jenkins
Merv *THE SWERVE* Davies

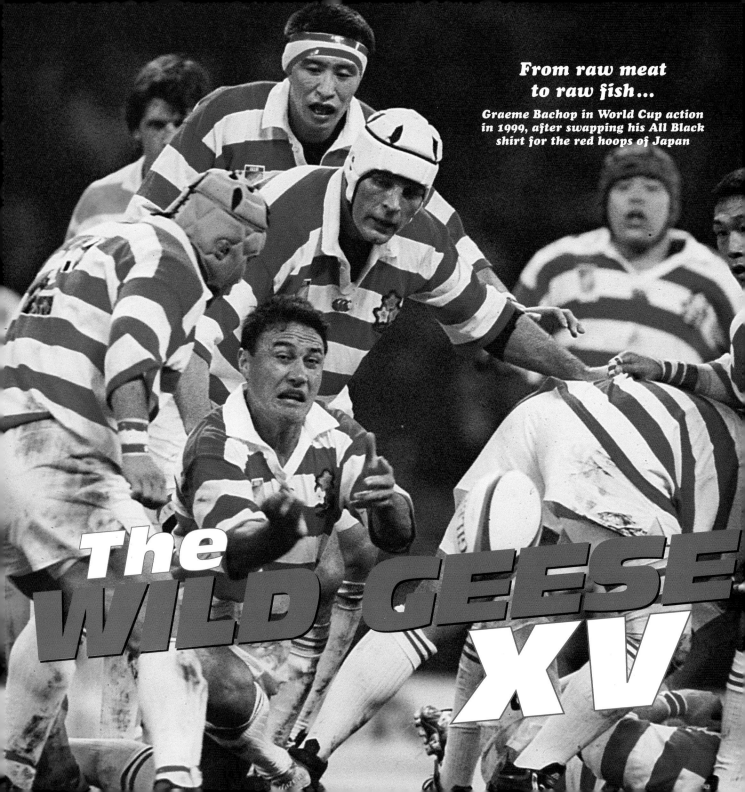

From raw meat
to raw fish...

Graeme Bachop in World Cup action
in 1999, after swapping his All Black
shirt for the red hoops of Japan

The
WILD GEESE
XV

VA'AIGA TUIGAMALA

SHANE HOWARTH

TANA UMAGA

JASON JONES-HUGHES

ANDREW McCORMICK

MIKE CATT

GRAEME BACHOP

TIAAN STRAUSS

JAMIE JOSEPH

MARTIN LESLIE

ABDELATIF BENAZZI

WILLIE OFAHENGAUE

PATRICIO NORIEGA

GREG SMITH

BRENDAN REIDY

O nce upon a time, you aspired to play rugby for the country of your birth. Now it seems you can play for anyone you like – as long as your Auntie Nelly once went there on a Saga holiday and sent you a postcard. Jack Charlton started the trend of dubious imports while manager of the Republic of Ireland soccer team; now professional rugby has taken up the baton big style, as this band of highly-paid mercenaries proves.

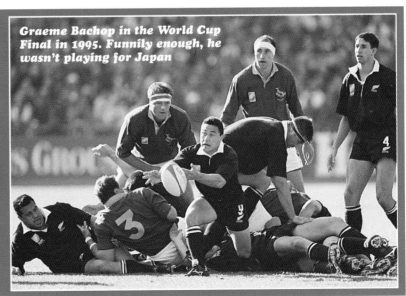

Graeme Bachop in the World Cup Final in 1995. Funnily enough, he wasn't playing for Japan

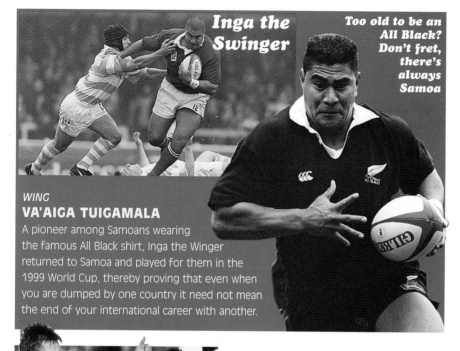

Inga the Swinger

Too old to be an All Black? Don't fret, there's always Samoa

WING
VA'AIGA TUIGAMALA

A pioneer among Samoans wearing the famous All Black shirt, Inga the Winger returned to Samoa and played for them in the 1999 World Cup, thereby proving that even when you are dumped by one country it need not mean the end of your international career with another.

FULL BACK
SHANE HOWARTH

Shane Howarth follows in a grand tradition of Welsh full backs – apart from his four caps for the All Blacks, of course. He qualifies to play for the Land Of Our Fathers on account of his great great uncle Eric's liking for leek pudding. Or something like that.

WING
TANA UMAGA

As a young boy in Samoa, Tama Umaga was in no doubt which team he wanted to play for when he grew up. Samoa? You must be joking! Why play for that bunch of losers when you can get on the next plane to Wellington and play for the best team in the world? The dreadlocked Umaga is now an All Black regular – even though his brother Mike still plays for Samoa.

CENTRE
JASON JONES-HUGHES

It beggars belief that anyone would want to play for Wales when they are, in fact, Australian – even if you do play the same position as Tim Horan. Centre Jason Jones-Hughes's strange desire to sport the red shirt meant that instead of

No more Argy bargy

One day he plays for Argentina...

The next he's a bloody Aussie

PROP
PATRICIO NORIEGA

After playing 22 Tests for one country, you can imagine that certain top players might get itchy feet and want to play for another. Such was the case with Patricio Noriega, once a mainstay of the Argentine front row with 22 caps, now proudly wearing the green and gold of Australia.

playing for the future World Champions, he spent most of the 1999 World Cup keeping a seat warm on the Dragons' subs bench while the Welsh and Aussie RFUs squabbled over how Wales had hi-jacked him into their ranks.

'I think I'm turning Japanese...'

Andrew McCormick – the only Jap with ginger hair and freckles

CENTRE
ANDREW McCORMICK

Kensuke Iwabuchi, Ryohei Miki, Tsutomu Matsuda, Patiliai Tuidraki – hardly names that roll off the typical rugby fan's tongue. Thank goodness, then, for Andrew McCormick, the New Zealand centre who captained Japan in the World Cup.

FLY HALF
MIKE CATT

The England selectors must have thought it was a great idea to have a South African in the team. What a pity the only one they could get was the invariably hopeless Mike Catt.

SCRUM HALF
GRAEME BACHOP

The World Cup must be a confusing time in the Bachop homestead. Scrum half Graeme played for New Zealand 31 times before cashing in on the dodgy three-year residency rules in order to join Japan. Meanwhile older brother Stephen, a former All Black fly half, now plays for Samoa. A rugby United Nations under one roof!

PROP
BRENDAN REIDY

New Zealander Reidy was getting nowhere in his quest to play for the All Blacks, so he had a brainwave: play for Samoa! He probably passed Jonah Lomu and Tana Umaga at Wellington airport.

SECOND ROW
ABDELATIF BENAZZI

Benazzi played against France for his native Morocco in a World Cup qualifier. He was so impressed with the opposition, he defected to Les Bleus and has been a cornerstone of their pack ever since.

HOOKER
GREG SMITH

Greg Smith played for Waikato in his native New Zealand. But, with Sean Fitzpatrick not only hooker but skipper of the All Blacks, Greg decided to cut his losses and went to play for Fiji instead, after discovering that his father once bought a coconut there. Smith was promptly made captain and led his team to the 1999 World Cup quarter-final play-offs.

SECOND ROW
WILLIE OFAHENGAUE

His crunching tackles have made flanker Willie O an Australian legend. However, the big man learned his rugby in the second row back in his native Tonga.

FLANKER
JAMIE JOSEPH

After stamping on Kyran Bracken's leg, New Zealander Jamie Joseph fled to Japan and appeared for them in World Cup 1999 – eight years after playing for the All Blacks in the 1991 World Cup.

FLANKER
MARTIN LESLIE

Just as his brother John dominates Scottish back play, so New Zealand-born Martin Leslie has added a dash of All Black steel to the Flower of Scotland.

NO. 8
TIAAN STRAUSS

Tiaan Strauss must have had mixed feelings as his team Australia knocked South Africa out of World Cup 1999. After all, before becoming an honorary Wallaby, Strauss won 15 caps for the Springboks.

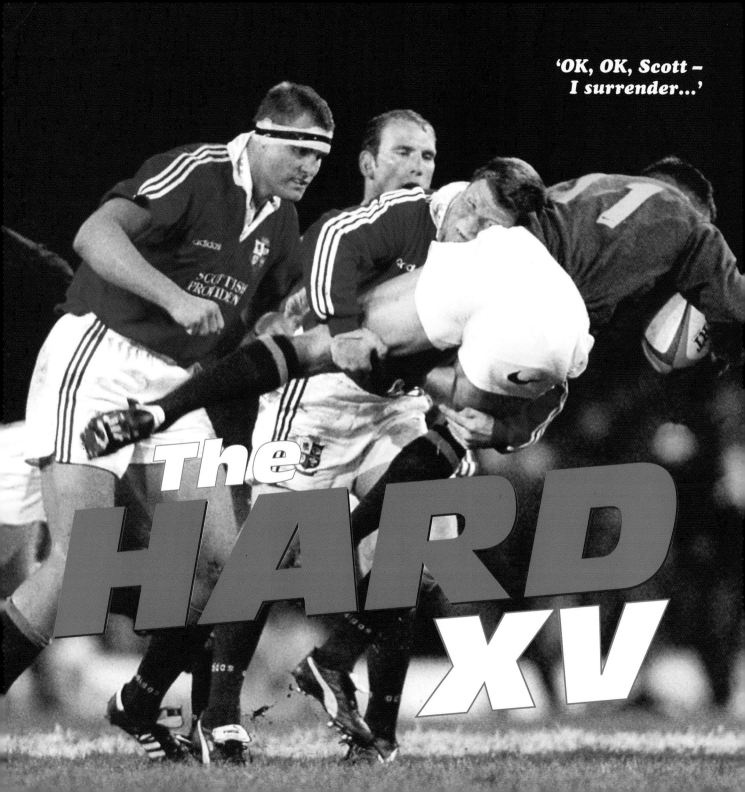

'OK, OK, Scott –
I surrender...'

The HARD XV

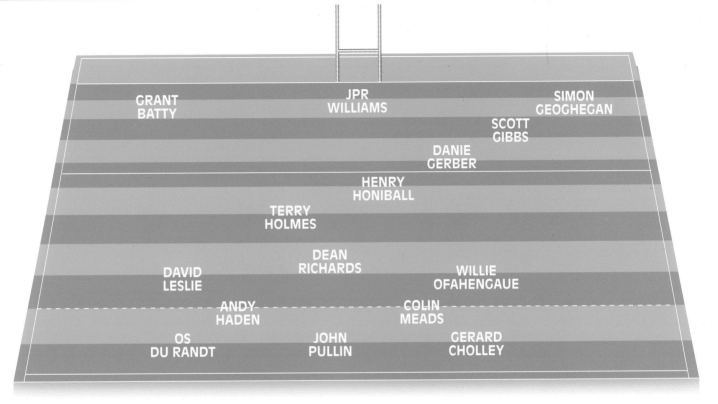

GRANT
BATTY

JPR
WILLIAMS

SIMON
GEOGHEGAN

SCOTT
GIBBS

DANIE
GERBER

HENRY
HONIBALL

TERRY
HOLMES

DEAN
RICHARDS

DAVID
LESLIE

WILLIE
OFAHENGAUE

ANDY
HADEN

COLIN
MEADS

OS
DU RANDT

JOHN
PULLIN

GERARD
CHOLLEY

Geoghegan's choirboy looks had the Aussies in a swoon

I t is a fact of life in rugby that no matter how many twinkle-toed geniuses you have in your team, you ain't going to win if they've been splattered into the mud. That's why every successful side has a subtle blend of skill and sheer brute force. Here are fifteen of the hardest cases ever to don a rugby shirt. Up against the Pretty Boys, we know where our money would be.

And the winner of 1975's Most Preposterous Sideburns of the Year Award goes to ... John Peter Rhys Williams of Cardiff

FULL BACK
JPR WILLIAMS

With his headband and quite sensational sideburns, JPR Williams was perhaps the most recognisable player of the 1970s. And even though it is 30 years since he made his debut for Wales, his impact on the pitch still reverberates.

Quite simply, JPR was nails. He didn't care how he stopped opponents as long as he did. His crunching tackles – the shoulder barge was his favourite – gave a new spin to the term flying winger. Neither did he stand on ceremony when

a fight broke out. During a mass brawl with the Springboks in 1974, JPR ran 30 yards in order to deliver a left hook to an opponent.

But he could take it as well as dishing it out: in the build-up to The Try (Barbarians v New Zealand 1973), JPR nearly had his head taken off by winger Bryan Williams, and the same thing happened when he scored his own try later in the match.

A 12-year Test career and 55 caps are testament to this remarkable player's staying power.

WING
GRANT BATTY

Pugnacious and redheaded, New Zealand's Grant Batty was the player everyone loved to hate during the 1970s. What's more, Batty didn't give a s***. The more he could wind up the whingeing Poms, Frogs and Aussies the better. A short man, he was quite capable of leaping like a salmon to tackle an opponent round the neck or connect with a crafty punch. But when he was not in your face, Batty was behind your try line. His little legs could carry him at quite phenomenal speeds and he was a supremely accomplished wingman. His try against the Barbarians in 1973, when he chipped over and retrieved his own kick as the boos rang out around the stadium, was a gem.

WING
SIMON GEOGHEGAN

Resembling the Tasmanian Devil in a green shirt, Irish winger Simon Geoghegan was an unforgettable sight as he raced down the wing with the ball in his hand. Hard, not to mention slightly bonkers, Geoghegan did not hide in the shadows; instead he actively went in search of the ball, diving head-first into rucks, strong-arming it with forwards and foraging like Peter Winterbottom on speed. At full frantic pace, he was almost impossible to stop, as he proved in scoring a superb try against England during a dramatic 13-12 Irish win at Twickenham in 1994.

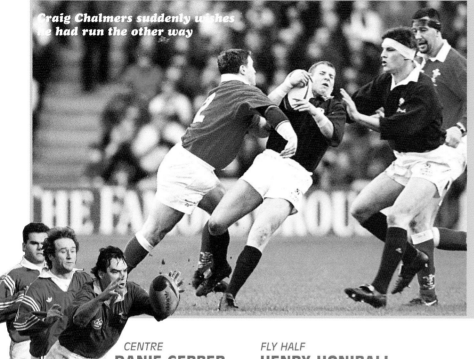

Craig Chalmers suddenly wishes he had run the other way

CENTRE
SCOTT GIBBS

Scott Gibbs was a pretty mean machine before he defected to rugby league in 1993. When he returned to union three years later, having been honed in the rock-hard 13-man game, Gibbs was nothing less than awesome. The South Africans discovered this to their cost when Gibbs spearheaded a no-nonsense British Lions back line in 1997. A crash tackle on 20-stone prop Os Du Randt sent the Springbok flying backwards and set the tone for a famous series win for the tourists. Remarkably fast for a big man, Gibbs has also scored some top tries, including the Five Nations rocket that sank England in 1999.

CENTRE
DANIE GERBER

Because of South Africa's international ban, most rugby fans were denied the chance of seeing Danie Gerber at his frightening best. So were most rugby players, much to their relief. Gerber was, to all intents and purposes, a Panzer tank in a green shirt: fast, unstoppable, and capable of destroying attackers at will.

Gerber single-handedly ripped England apart at Ellis Park in 1984, scoring three blistering tries in a 35-9 romp.

In Invitational XV matches staged in Europe he was invariably the star of the show, and gave crowds a tantalising taste of his brilliance.

FLY HALF
HENRY HONIBALL

In the International Union of Non-tackling Fly Halves (President: B John), South Africa's Henry Honiball is most definitely regarded as a scab.

Sadly, however, the days of willowy poet-like No.10s who don't get their shorts dirty are long gone. Honiball is part of the new breed who wear shoulder pads. Standing at well over six feet and built like a Transvaal outhouse, he revels in diving at the feet of rampaging back-row forwards and scavenging at breakdowns like a crazed wildebeest at a waterhole.

It may not be cricket for those purists brought up on the mercurial skills of Kyle, Morgan, John and Bennett, but in the 100 mph professional game it is the future.

SCRUM HALF
TERRY HOLMES

If it hadn't been for a series of crippling injuries, Terry Holmes could have become as great a Welsh scrum half as his predecessor Gareth Edwards. Then again, if he hadn't been such a hard nut on the pitch, he wouldn't have spent so much time on the treatment table. Whereas Edwards preferred to dart and snipe around back rows, Holmes enjoyed bludgeoning his way straight through them, the more the merrier. Indeed, at times it seemed that Wales were playing with a fourth back-row man – which annoyed his fly half Gareth Davies no end. One Lions appearance and 25 Wales caps are moderate reward for an outstanding tough guy – but an indication of how injury wrecked his career.

PROP
OS DU RANDT

Weighing in at over 20 stone, former South African commando Os Du Randt is not the most agile of prop forwards – but when he gets on a rumble it takes something special to arrest him (namely Scott Gibbs). 'The Ox' has overcome many career-threatening injuries, and is a tough cookie off the pitch as well. He recently survived a spectacular car crash and came back more terrifying than ever.

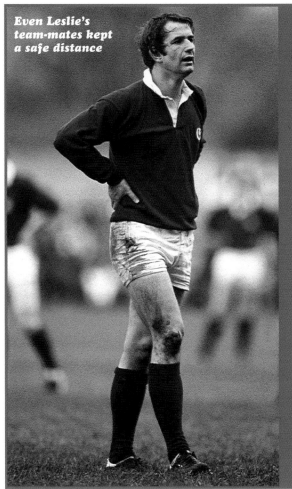

Even Leslie's team-mates kept a safe distance

FLANKER
DAVID LESLIE

The polite word for it is commitment. But, quite simply, Scotland flanker David Leslie was a nutter. It didn't matter where the ball was on the pitch, he would go after it – usually head first. Even when he retired in 1985, Leslie refused to relinquish his lovingly-cultivated hard man tag. Invited to appear in an old boys' match at Glenalmond College, near Perth, Leslie proceeded to play like a man possessed. The body count among the youngsters was so high that the master in charge was forced to stop the game and plead with Leslie to calm down.

PROP
GERARD CHOLLEY

Of all the grizzled hard men to play in the French, or indeed any, front row, Gerard Cholley was perhaps the hardest. Rarely a match went by without the former paratrooper inflicting some form of physical damage on his opponents. His finest hour came during a match against Scotland at Paris in 1977. Cholley began

the afternoon by laying out No. 8 Don McDonald with a savage haymaker. For the rest of the game, he systematically went on to let his fists do the talking with the remainder of the Scottish pack, prompting one observer to compare him to "a bus conductor proceeding up the aisle taking fares". Amazingly, Cholley wasn't sent off. Mind you, the ref was probably scared of him too.

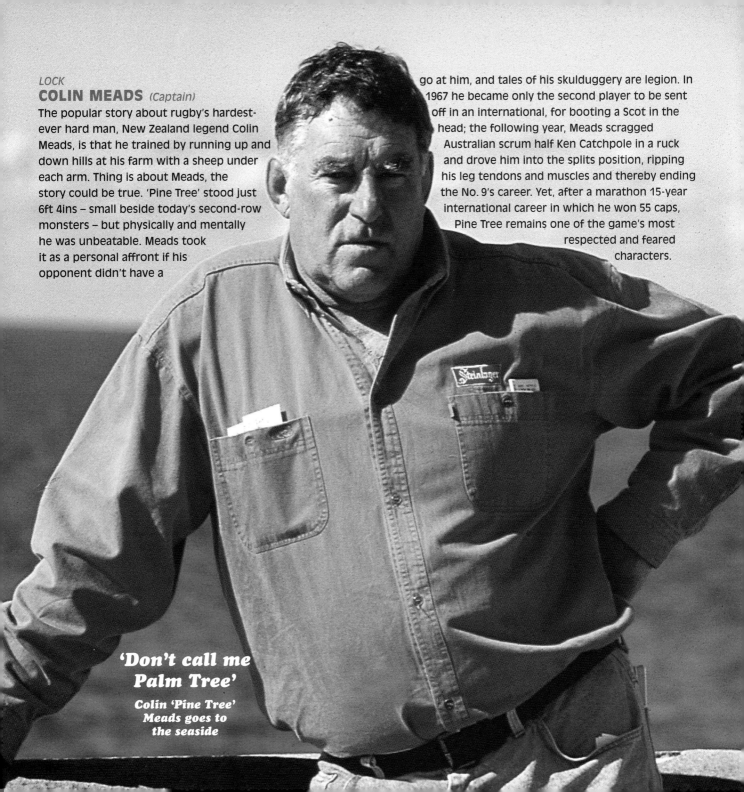

LOCK
COLIN MEADS (Captain)

The popular story about rugby's hardest-ever hard man, New Zealand legend Colin Meads, is that he trained by running up and down hills at his farm with a sheep under each arm. Thing is about Meads, the story could be true. 'Pine Tree' stood just 6ft 4ins – small beside today's second-row monsters – but physically and mentally he was unbeatable. Meads took it as a personal affront if his opponent didn't have a go at him, and tales of his skulduggery are legion. In 1967 he became only the second player to be sent off in an international, for booting a Scot in the head; the following year, Meads scragged Australian scrum half Ken Catchpole in a ruck and drove him into the splits position, ripping his leg tendons and muscles and thereby ending the No. 9's career. Yet, after a marathon 15-year international career in which he won 55 caps, Pine Tree remains one of the game's most respected and feared characters.

'Don't call me
Palm Tree'

Colin 'Pine Tree'
Meads goes to
the seaside

HOOKER
JOHN PULLIN

It takes a special kind of toughness to preside over one of the most dismal periods in English rugby, yet still inspire the side to two of the most remarkable upsets in the game. Bristol farmer John Pullin had it in spades. Captain of England during the barren 1970s, Pullin overcame the fact that the rest of his team were crap to win 42 caps, as well as seven for the Lions. He also captained the team to away victories over New Zealand and South Africa – no mean feat when one considers England in those days would be hard pressed to give a half-decent Third XV a game. Hard, uncompromising, and with a heart of oak, Pullin was a real hero.

LOCK
ANDY HADEN

We make no apologies for including another All Black legend in our Hard XV second row – they must breed 'em that way in New Zealand. Just when opposition locks thought it was safe to venture out following the retirement of Colin Meads, along came Andy Haden. Equally hard, Haden not only regarded anyone who wasn't a Kiwi as a poofter but also believed in victory at all costs. With seconds left in a match against Wales in 1978, Haden realised that the All Blacks needed a penalty to win. The big man duly took an outrageous dive at the next lineout. Penalty secured, the Blacks won 13-12.

Haden had the best cauliflower ear but the worst 'tache

Deano really needed to go on a first aid course ... and so did his opponents

DEAN RICHARDS

When things looked to be getting a bit sticky and the opposition appeared to be getting the upper hand, there was nothing more comforting for an England supporter than the chant "Dean-o, Dean-o" ringing round Twickenham and the sight of big Dean Richards wrapping his considerable mitts around the ball. The shambling Leicester No. 8 looked like he'd just fallen out of bed most of the time, but Deano was the rock upon which England's glory years of the 1990s were founded. Phenomenal strength and spooky anticipation, combined with an iron will to succeed, not only made him one of the great No. 8s, but a cult hero at Welford Road and Twickers. Deano also had a healthy disrespect for the modern culture of rugby athletes. He enjoyed a few beers the night before an international – drinking until 6 am on the day of 1995 Third Place play-off – and his reaction to receiving a motivation tape from England manager Geoff Cooke was to throw it straight in the bin.

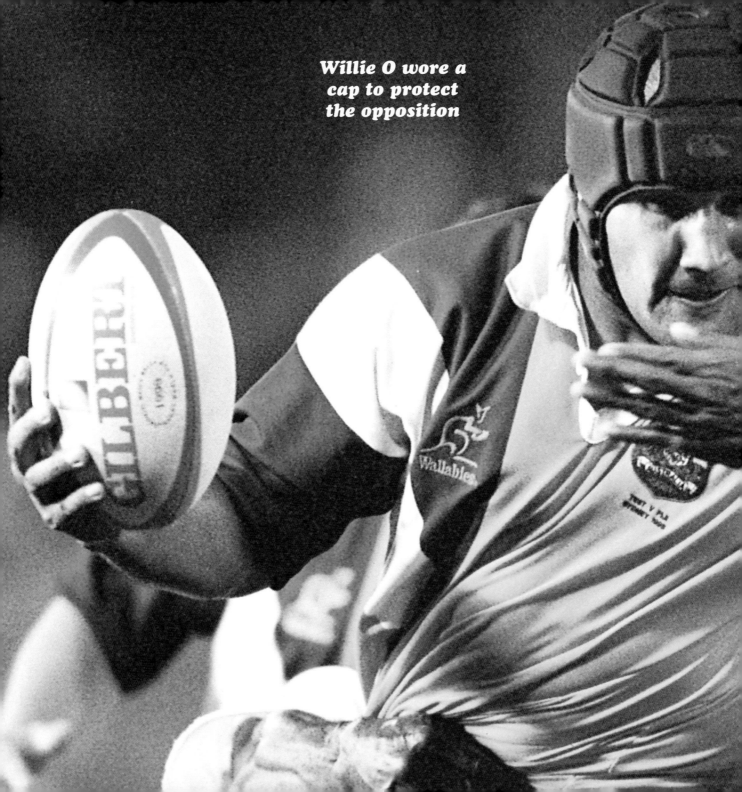

Willie O wore a
cap to protect
the opposition

FLANKER
WILLIE OFAHENGAUE

It was the opening play of the 1990 Bledisloe Cup match between Australia and New Zealand, and the ball was with legendary Kiwi flanker Alan Whetton. Suddenly, from nowhere, a gold-shirted missile struck Whetton in the midriff, knocking him several feet backwards and forcing him to spill the ball. Meet Willie Ofahengaue, the Tongan-born flanker who, with that debut hit, announced himself on the world stage as a hard man to be reckoned with. At his peak in the early 1990s, before injury took its toll, Willie O was one of the most fearsome and feared back-row men in the game, defensively devastating and able to make yards of ground with the ball in his meaty hands. As Whetton nursed his bruised ribs that day, he no doubt reflected ironically that Willie O had originally toured Australia as an All Black colt – until an over-zealous customs official refused to let him back into the country, and he defected to the Wallabies.

'Look, I'm going back to union and you can't stop me!'

Scott Quinnell fights off the attentions of Dennis Betts in the 1995 Rugby League World Cup clash between Wales and England. Four years later Quinnell would be turning out for Wales in the Rugby Union World Cup

THEY CROSSED GREAT

THE DIVIDE

These days, the traffic between rugby league and union tends to be a one-way procession south, as stars of the 13-man game search for lucrative contracts with Harlequins, Bath or Saracens. But in the

days when the only payment for playing union was a pat on the back and a ticket for free pie and chips, many top stars such as David Bishop (above) found the lure of the chequebook impossible to resist. Here, then, are 15 of the finest players to have played both sides of the great North-South divide.

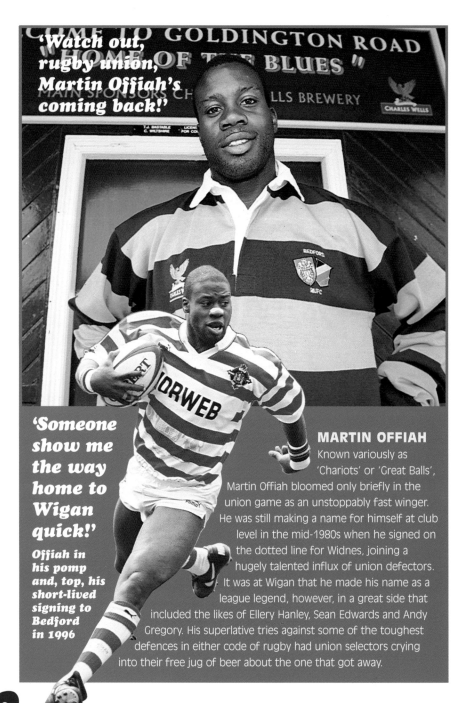

'Watch out, rugby union, Martin Offiah's coming back!'

'Someone show me the way home to Wigan quick!'

Offiah in his pomp and, top, his short-lived signing to Bedford in 1996

MARTIN OFFIAH

Known variously as 'Chariots' or 'Great Balls', Martin Offiah bloomed only briefly in the union game as an unstoppably fast winger. He was still making a name for himself at club level in the mid-1980s when he signed on the dotted line for Widnes, joining a hugely talented influx of union defectors. It was at Wigan that he made his name as a league legend, however, in a great side that included the likes of Ellery Hanley, Sean Edwards and Andy Gregory. His superlative tries against some of the toughest defences in either code of rugby had union selectors crying into their free jug of beer about the one that got away.

DAVID BISHOP

As a youngster, David Bishop was one of the most promising scrum halves to come out of Wales, with greatness predicted for him. Sadly for the Welsh, Bishop had already decided that the prospect of a steady wage packet from the Rugby League was preferable to poverty in the valleys. He duly went north and became an inspirational player for, among others, Hull KR.

ALLAN BATEMAN

Alongside Scott Gibbs, former league exile Allan Bateman makes a formidable partnership in the Welsh midfield. And like so many others who have returned to union after learning the disciplines of the 13-man game, he has become a player transformed. Bateman now plays for Northampton after a spell in league during which, among other teams, he strutted his stuff for Cronulla in the Australian league.

TERRY HOLMES

In many ways Terry Holmes' game was far better suited to league. As scrum half for Wales, he always preferred to play as a fourth flanker. After a career in union that was littered with injuries, Bradford Northern decided to take the risk of buying him up. Holmes, accepting that he had to try and make some money from the last few years of his playing life, went north. Inevitably, his catalogue of injuries continued to curtail his league career until he was forced into retirement.

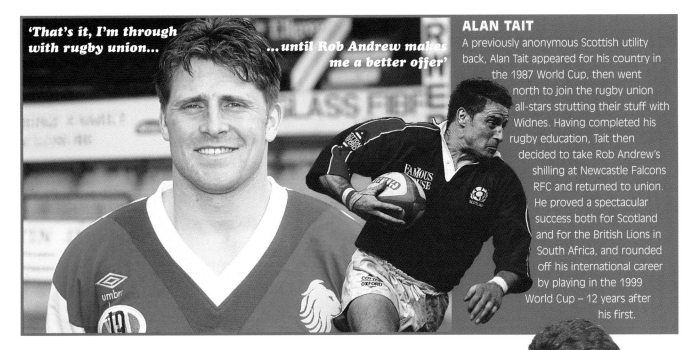

'That's it, I'm through with rugby union...

...until Rob Andrew makes me a better offer'

ALAN TAIT

A previously anonymous Scottish utility back, Alan Tait appeared for his country in the 1987 World Cup, then went north to join the rugby union all-stars strutting their stuff with Widnes. Having completed his rugby education, Tait then decided to take Rob Andrew's shilling at Newcastle Falcons RFC and returned to union. He proved a spectacular success both for Scotland and for the British Lions in South Africa, and rounded off his international career by playing in the 1999 World Cup – 12 years after his first.

PAUL MORIARTY

A fearsome and feisty customer for Wales, Paul Moriarty was ideally suited to the combative world of rugby league. And following the 1987 World Cup, the blond-haired flanker realised that the money Salford were dangling in front of certain Welsh players was too good to resist. He duly packed his bags and headed north to enjoy a successful, if never spectacular, career in the 13-man code.

JONATHAN DAVIES

The most high-profile defector to league was the brilliant Jonathan Davies. A gifted fly half, he had the misfortune to play in one of the lousiest Wales teams of all time. Yet almost singlehanded in 1988, he led them to a Triple Crown and a famous victory over England. That summer, however, Wales were thrashed during a tour to New Zealand and, disillusioned, Davies legged it north to Widnes. It took him a while to settle into his new code, but when he did – clearly benefiting from a few sessions on the weights – he established himself as a league great, representing Great Britain with huge success. Upon his return to union – the first defector ever to be allowed back – in 1997 aged 33, he remarkably won three more caps for Wales, including one against England.

England rugby union debutant Barrie-Jon Mather, right, looks back fondly on his rugby league days – when he actually got his hands on the ball once in a while

BARRIE-JON MATHER

Named after the great Welsh union fly half, Barrie-Jon Mather nevertheless pursued a highly successful career in league with Castleford and Wigan. But with a dearth of backs in the union game, he spotted the chance for some glory by changing codes during the winter recess in Superleague. He signed for Sale and, largely on the strength of his league reputation, muscled his way into the England squad. Although he did get a run-out in the defeat against Wales in the 1999 Five Nations, his limitations were there for all to see and he was omitted from England's World Cup squad.

JOHN DEVEREUX

A bullocking Welsh centre in the mode of Gravell and Gibbs, John Devereux was among the defectors who went north after the 1987 World Cup, despite being one of his team's top performers and a try-scorer in the quarter-final win over England. He became a solid member of the Salford side before returning to union in 1997 to finish off his career with ambitious Worcester.

JASON ROBINSON

League livewire Jason Robinson was another who had union clubs drooling with anticipation of acquiring his signature. Eventually it was Bath who signed him – but twinkle-toed Robinson was a huge disappointment. The likeable winger scored spectacular tries for Wigan and Great Britain, but for some reason could not provide the same moments of glory for the faithful at the Rec.

GARY CONNOLLY

As soon as the laws preventing players skipping between codes were disposed of in 1996, Wigan's blond-haired centre Gary Connolly became a ripe target for union sides, and in particular big-spending Harlequins, who saw him as an ideal foil for Will Carling. Two of the biggest names in either code duly lined up in the Quins' midfield. But for some reason, Connolly was unable to make the same impact in union as he had in league. A big disappointment for Quins – and for England, who had grand ideas about the league man turning out for the national side.

SCOTT QUINNELL

The loss of rising star Scott Quinnell to Wigan in 1994 was a grievous body-blow to the Welsh Union, and one which took many years to get over. Indeed, it was only with Quinnell's return four years later that the Welsh side were able to resurrect themselves. His charging runs soon made him a favourite with crowds at Central Park and turned him from a great into an exceptional player back in the union fold.

John Bentley in his second spell as an England rugby union player and, below, playing league for Leeds

JOHN BENTLEY

One of the first English rugby mercenaries, 'Bentos' went north for the money with Leeds RLFC, then came back to union with the ultimate mercenaries' club – Rob Andrew's Newcastle – when the game turned professional. Bentley had failed to make much of an impression when first playing for England, but his spell in league transformed him beyond belief, and his new power and speed made him an astute choice for the British Lions party which toured South Africa in 1997. Bentley's 80-yard try against Gauteng was the best of the tour and cemented a remarkable return to the union game.

"Fran Cotton knew the league players' professionalism would be vital to the Lions tour. From day one, we trained with the intensity at which we desired to play – which came as a bit of a surprise to some of the rugby union lads."
– *JOHN BENTLEY, Lions Uncaged*

DAVID WATKINS

The mastermind behind Welsh Five Nations successes in the mid-'60s, and a British Lions captain to boot, fly half David Watkins turned his back on union for a lucrative contract with Salford. He shocked the Welsh establishment, but served notice that in impoverished areas of the country the lure of northern chequebooks would always provide an incentive for top players to change code. He also proved that union players could thrive in the hurly-burly of the 13-man game, playing successfully for Great Britain.

SCOTT GIBBS

Another to benefit from the tougher training regimes of league, Scott Gibbs left union for St Helens as one of its more devastating players and returned to it three years later well-nigh unstoppable for Swansea and Wales. Like John Bentley, Gibbs thrived for the Lions amid the hard men of South Africa where his tough tackling and thunderous runs blasted holes in the opposition. And with his splendid match-winning try against England in the 1999 Five Nations, Gibbs proved that he was not just a Panzer tank.

"When I got my first Test jersey for Scotland, that was the moment when I realised I would never be an All Black. I must admit there was a bit of sadness in me then."
JOHN LESLIE

"I'm pleased to say I don't think about rugby all the time; just most of the time."
LAWRENCE DALLAGLIO

"We said before the game that we were not going to get involved in any fisticuffs."
– COLIN CHARVIS of Wales, after being banned for brawling with Roberto Grau in the showpiece opening game

"If you're being poked in the eye or punched in the face, you act accordingly. Some back off, some go for the blood."
– SCOTT GIBBS defending Colin Charvis

"For anyone to score four tries at Lansdowne Road is special. Before that USA game, he was like a coiled spring waiting to explode."
Ireland coach WARREN GATLAND on cult hero Keith Wood

WORLD CUP

"They scored, so we scored. There is nothing like a Samoan rugby player with his back to the wall, especially one who has been told all week they are going to be demolished. Wales forgot they haven't beaten us for 14 years. We might not be good in the scrum, nor in the lineout, but at the arts of pure rugby we went out to show there is nothing like a Samoan."

Samoa captain PAT LAM after the 38-31 win against Wales

"If one of our players is on the floor and getting punched in the face by one of their players, I'm not going to stand off."
– England captain MARTIN JOHNSON

"I went for the ball, not the guy's head, but Joost van der Westhuizen took it away at the last moment."
– BRENDAN VENTER of South Africa, sent off for stamping on Martin Panizza

"Everything was against us: we got stuck in the traffic, the police escort didn't work properly, the boys were dehydrated and the officials gave us 15 minutes' grace rather than the half hour we wanted. What am I meant to tell my guys? That the Europeans hate the Polynesians?"
– Tonga coach DAVE WATERSON after losing 101-10 to England

TALK SHOW

"It would be nice if, when we consistently win the ball, they learn to catch the pass."
– *French hooker RAPHAEL IBANEZ on the French backs*

"Scotland is the Pacific nation of Britain."
VA'AIGA TUIGAMALA of Samoa

"It's really difficult to play against sides like Spain and Uruguay because they're so poor."
South African coach NICK MALLETT

"When I do the Haka, I feel that the presence of the past, future and present All Blacks are with me. Spiritually it gives me such an adrenalin rush that I'd run into a brick wall."
JONAH LOMU

"He is one of ours and we would like to have him on our side, for sure. But then so would every side."
FE'AO VUNIPOLA of Tonga on Lomu

"As I tipped over and started to come down, I knew I could be in big trouble. I was so relieved when I could feel everything was in working order."
England full back MATT PERRY after being tackled in midair by Tonga's Isi Tapueluelu

"Being in the front row, I reckon I know a hell of a lot more about what's going on than the referee."
Fiji hooker GREG SMITH after France were awarded a crucial penalty try

"I expect the bruises, but the old body's holding up. After the game against Tonga I had to ice my ankles up, but that's usual. By Thursday I'm usually back to normal."
JOSH 'Crock' KRONFELD of New Zealand

"This was the first time I have ever had to try to stop him. I will not be disappointed if it is the last."
JEREMY GUSCOTT

"I guess there was something he didn't like about me."
JONAH LOMU on being punched by Lawrence Dallaglio after he touched down

97

FORWARDS

Yes, we all know it's called a brick shithouse, but Bill McLaren insists on calling it a brick outhouse. Here's eight forwards who would never be allowed in a lift together – eight monsters you wouldn't like to meet on a dark night ... or indeed on a sunny day.

The BRICK OUTHOUSE VIII

IAIN MILNE

Iain Milne was known as The Bear – though The Brick Oothoose would have been more appropriate for the giant 19-stone prop. A fearsome scrummager, his sheer size helped secure the shaky Scotland scrum and allow the likes of John Jeffrey and David Leslie to fly off and create havoc among opposition backs. In his last international in 1990, Milne scrummed down with his hooker brother Kenny.

NAKA DROTSKE

One member of a fearsome South African front row including Os Du Randt and Adrian Garvey, Naka Drotske sounds like a particularly painful type of Japanese torture and, as international hookers will testify, he plays like one as well. Drotske weighs in at well over 18st, yet scrummages like a little demon.

CRAIG QUINNELL

When your dad is legendary Welsh flanker Derek Quinnell, a career as a bruising back-five forward is fairly inevitable. So it was for young Scott and Craig Quinnell, who emerged from the Valleys to terrify oppositions around the world. Scott was first on the scene, but if anything his younger brother Craig (left) was the more imposing. Clearly when it came to eating Weetabix in the Quinnell household, he was first at the breakfast table. A monster outhouse on his own, but in tandem with his brother, awesome.

OLIVIER ROUMAT

Standing 6ft 7in and weighing over 19 stone, France colossus Olivier Roumat would be hard pressed to even get inside a brick outhouse. Just to make things even more unfair for his opponents, Roumat was originally a basketball player – which means he has hands and co-ordination better than some of the vaunted French backs.

ROBERT PAPAREMBORDE

As Mike Burton succinctly put it: "If Paparemborde has a neck, then there's no way of telling." The French prop's brute strength made him one of the most feared front-rowers of the 1970s. The fact he was also a judo black belt was just one more very sensible reason not to mess with big Paparemborde.

FRIK DU PREEZ

A legend in South Africa in the 1960s, big Frik Du Preez dominated any forward battle he chose. The sight of Du Preez plucking the ball out of the air and galloping through the lineout at some quaking fly half had Springbok fans rubbing their hands with glee. Yet Du Preez was a laid-back dude off the pitch. While his dour team-mates plotted victory at all costs, the big second row couldn't give a toss – and retired in 1971 to run a farm in the Kalahari Desert.

LAURENT RODRIGUES

The Bull of Dax, Laurent Rodrigues was one of the most terrifying players ever to don the No.8 shirt. Huge in size and strength, it would take at least three men to drag him down – and then only if one of them was armed with an elephant gun. He was instrumental in the famous French win over New Zealand in 1986, a match in which Buck Shelford needed 22 stitches in his shattered scrotum and several New Zealand colleagues required new shorts. In an era when coach Jacques Fouroux liked to field enormous packs, Rodrigues was one of the giants.

ERIC CHAMP

If Seventies pop star Leo Sayer had undergone a metamorphosis into the Incredible Hulk, he would have looked like French flank forward Eric Champ. Like Jean-Pierre Rives, Champ was distinctive for his flowing locks and for his iron-like tackling – except Champ was three times the size of Rives and 246 times as ugly. He was a mainstay of the 1987 France Grand Slam team, scoring a couple of tries in their clinching victory over Ireland, and playing a huge part in their march to the World Cup Final. In the 1991 World Cup encounter with England, Champ set out his stall early, burying winger Nigel Heslop beneath a barrage of haymakers and forcing him to leave the pitch.

FORWARDS

Until recently, even the fittest forward would be left gasping for air if they had to run more than 10 yards. The modern breed, however, are built to run and run. Here are eight non-stop players you wouldn't want to play extra time against.

The DURACELL VIII

JOSH KRONFELD

New Zealand pocket dynamo Josh Kronfeld just keeps on running. It's said that at half-time, the All Blacks simply lift Kronfeld's scrum cap and top him up with 4-star. All performers occasionally need to come into the pit lane, however, and in the latter stages of World Cup '99, Kronfeld looked in need of a service. The frightening thing is that like a finely-tuned Ferrari, he will be back to terrorise opponents next season.

PAT LAM
(right)

It would be unfair to call Samoa a one-man team – but what the hell. Without the inspirational Pat Lam, it is unlikely the men from the South Seas would have made an impact on the world stage at Wales '99. The abiding image is of their fantastic victory over the Welsh at Cardiff, a win sealed by Lam himself. Having virtually single-handedly subdued the monster Welsh back row, Lam then made a monkey out of goalkicking king Neil Jenkins by intercepting a pass and racing away for 80 untouched yards to score the vital try.

NEIL BACK (below)

England's Neil Back is the kind of player who, after covering every blade of grass at Twickenham for 80 minutes, runs all the way home to Leicester. Officials have given up checking Back for drug abuse – instead they test to see if he is actually the T1000 cyborg from Terminator. Supremely fit, fast and ferrety, Back would probably play all 15 positions on the park at the same time if he had the chance. He has finally made the England open side his own, and not a moment too soon. Even All Black coach John Hart admitted that Back would be the only England player he would have in his team.

CHRISTIAN CALIFANO

Some players just aren't fair. If Jonah Lomu springs to mind in the backs, then his forward equivalent has to be Christian Califano. The French prop can run 100 metres in 12 seconds, can pass like a back, kick like a mule and sidestep like Barry John. Yet he can also scrummage as well as any traditional member of the front row union. His technique is rock solid – it's just that he is also like a hippo on speed in the loose, which makes him one of the finest front row men to ever play the game.

OLIVIER MAGNE

It was the greatest match ever seen, and at the heart of France's historic win over New Zealand in the 1999 World Cup semi-final was skipper Olivier Magne. Another to sport a distinctive scrumcap – his was a fetching white-and-blue style – Magne was not only deep in every ruck and maul, but he still had the stamina to kick and chase the ball 80 yards to create a dramatic late score for Philippe Bernat-Salles. In the final, France were subdued – except for Magne, who refused to lay down even when his nose was splattered all over his face.

RUBEN KRUGER

While golden boy Bobby Skinstad was making all the headlines and coming up with none of the goods during World Cup '99, it was left to Ruben Kruger to crank up the South African back row with his non-stop, all-action version of the game. Like all the best flankers – Back, Kronfeld – Kruger prefers to let his hits and his ball-winning do the talking, which was just as well with the illustrious Skinstad out to lunch for much of the tournament.

LAWRENCE DALLAGLIO

After months of careful preparation for World Cup 1999, England finally revealed that their one killer move was, er … give it to Dallaglio. Kick-offs, scrums, lineouts, back moves – it didn't matter. The ball was invariably given to England's disgraced former captain, who appeared to be repenting for his drug shame by taking on every single opponent himself. Mind you, big Lol never failed to make the hard yards. After a traumatic year, his was a performance of sheer defiance.

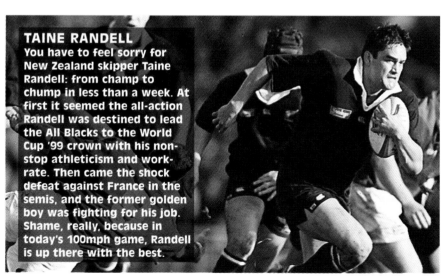

TAINE RANDELL
You have to feel sorry for New Zealand skipper Taine Randell: from champ to chump in less than a week. At first it seemed the all-action Randell was destined to lead the All Blacks to the World Cup '99 crown with his non-stop athleticism and work-rate. Then came the shock defeat against France in the semis, and the former golden boy was fighting for his job. Shame, really, because in today's 100mph game, Randell is up there with the best.

Catching the ball 1

Catching the ball 2

FORWARDS

Nobody really minds an outbreak of spontaneous handbags at five paces. But there are some things that take place on a rugby field which are beyond the pale and belong in the zoo. Here are eight players who would probably prefer raw meat to an orange at half-time.

The ANIMAL VIII

FRANCK TOURNAIRE

As the victorious French team did a lap of honour after their famous victory over New Zealand in the 1999 World Cup semi-final, 18-stone prop Franck Tournaire brought tears to everyone's eyes as he carried his young daughter on his shoulders. Earlier, however, it was All Black skipper Taine Randell who was in tears after having his ear bitten – with loving dad Tournaire the alleged culprit. Although Tournaire was cleared, video evidence appears to show the Frenchman enjoying a tasty snack. He was not alone: Josh Kronfeld claimed he had been gouged in the eye, Anton Oliver headbutted and Byron Kelleher bitten. A week later in the final, Australian skipper John Eales threatened to take his side off the pitch if the French persisted with eye gouging.

KEVIN YATES

With still some time to go before the final whistle of their cup tie against London Scottish at the Recreation Ground, peckish Bath prop Kevin Yates decided he couldn't wait for the post-match steak pie and chips. Instead, he decided to tuck into the nearest available slab of meat – which so happened to be his opponent Simon Fenn's ear. Fenn was led from the pitch in agony and later required 28 stitches in his mangled lug (right). Yates, who to this day protests his innocence, was banned for six months and later moved to New Zealand to play rugby.

PAUL VAN ZANDVLIET

Newcastle Falcons' giant prop Paul Van Zandvliet is known as 'Tank', and he obviously wanted a top-up when he appeared to take a huge bite out of Leicester flanker Neil Back's skull during a league match in 1997. Had Van Zandvliet followed through with his enormous chomp, he would have eaten half of Back's brain. However, the Newcastle man avoided punishment after he managed to convince a disciplinary committee that his actions were purely accidental.

NGALU TAUFO'OU

One can perhaps excuse Tongan winger Isi Tapueluelu for over-exuberance as he speared into England's mid-air full back Matt Perry during the two teams' World Cup quarter-final play-off. Not, however, his prop colleague Ngalu Taufo'ou. Following the outrageous challenge, Perry landed sickeningly on his neck. Immediately, a punch-up ensued which flanker Richard Hill was innocently trying to simmer down. From nowhere, the 20-stone Taufo'ou raced across and took out the burly Hill with a thunderous punch. The referee, standing just yards away, had no option but to send him off.

GARY REES

Former England flanker Gary Rees was a fiery competitor. But this is no excuse for his actions during a match between his club Nottingham and London Irish in the early 1990s. Fed up of being obstructed in the lineout, Rees turned round and broke opposition back-rower Stefan Marty's jaw with a vicious punch. Marty later sued Rees and won damages.

ROBERTO GRAU

The picture should have been of Shirley Bassey, or at least Neil Jenkins. Instead the abiding image of the opening match of the 1999 World Cup was of Argentina's prop Roberto Grau with his fingers stuck halfway inside Welshman Garin Jenkins' eye socket. Grau was later suspended – but for a dust-up with Colin Charvis. Remarkably, he escaped punishment for what appeared to be blatant eye-gouging.

THE CANTERBURY PACK

Your average pack has at least one nutter guaranteed to get into a punch-up. But in the Canterbury pack of 1971, all eight were psychos. Against the touring British Lions, they gave Sandy Carmichael such a merciless pounding that the Scottish prop suffered five fractures of his cheek-bone and was flown home. In the days before citing and video evidence, not one of his opponents was brought to book.

RICHARD LOE

No-nonsense New Zealand prop Richard Loe was not a man to cross. So when Australian winger Paul Carrozza had the audacity to score a try during a hotly-contested Bledisloe Cup game, there could be only one outcome. Loe duly crunched into the hapless Wallaby after the touchdown, breaking his nose.

BACKS

There are few more thrilling sights in rugby than a speed merchant at full throttle. This seven would give Linford Christie a run for his money.

The ROAD RUNNER VII

RORY UNDERWOOD

Who knows how many tries England's Rory Underwood would have scored if, during his early international career, someone had passed him the ball. As it was, he still ended up with an English record of 49. At his prime, he was the most devastating finisher in the game with more than enough pace to burn off the quickest cover defence. Five tries against Fiji in 1989 are evidence of that, as was the spectacular second-half hat-trick he scored against the Irish in 1988 – for many, his finest match in England colours.

BRENDAN MULLIN

When Brendan Mullin broke the Irish 110-metres hurdles record in 1986, a great career beckoned in international athletics. Instead, Mullin turned to rugby. It was a decision which defences around the world cursed for 11 years. Incredibly quick, Mullin nevertheless played most of his games for Ireland in the centre. It is testament to his ability to see, then race through, the gap, that he notched up an Irish record of 17 tries and won 50 caps for his country.

CHRISTIAN CULLEN

It was no surprise that the only person capable of catching Christophe Dominici as he seemed destined to score against New Zealand was Christian Cullen. Shamefully wasted in the centre, Cullen's searing pace makes him one of the world's most devastating attacking full backs. Cullen's secret is his ability to combine speed with balance and a scary eye for the break. At his best – or rather in his best position – he is lethal.

ANDREW HARRIMAN

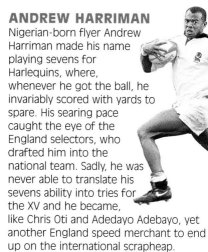

Nigerian-born flyer Andrew Harriman made his name playing sevens for Harlequins, where, whenever he got the ball, he invariably scored with yards to spare. His searing pace caught the eye of the England selectors, who drafted him into the national team. Sadly, he was never able to translate his sevens ability into tries for the XV and he became, like Chris Oti and Adedayo Adebayo, yet another England speed merchant to end up on the international scrapheap.

JJ WILLIAMS

Gerald Davies got more of the plaudits – but few would have bet against JJ Williams in a straight race between the two Welsh wingers. Thin as a whippet and just as fast, JJ scored some spectacular tries for Wales and the Lions during an illustrious career. Many people recall Graham Price's dramatic try against France in 1975, but most forget it was JJ, racing 100 yards across the muddy turf, who reached the ball first and set up the score for the Pontypool prop.

CHRISTOPHE DOMINICI

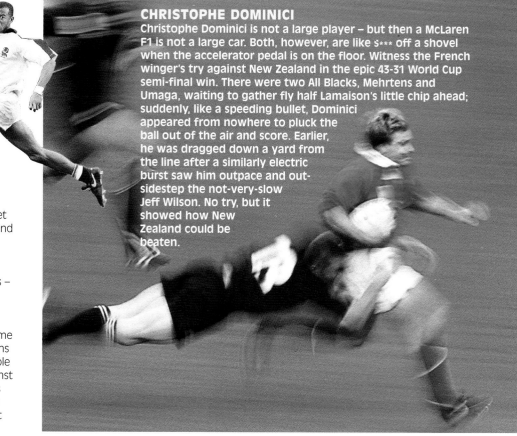

Christophe Dominici is not a large player – but then a McLaren F1 is not a large car. Both, however, are like s*** off a shovel when the accelerator pedal is on the floor. Witness the French winger's try against New Zealand in the epic 43-31 World Cup semi-final win. There were two All Blacks, Mehrtens and Umaga, waiting to gather fly half Lamaison's little chip ahead; suddenly, like a speeding bullet, Dominici appeared from nowhere to pluck the ball out of the air and score. Earlier, he was dragged down a yard from the line after a similarly electric burst saw him outpace and out-sidestep the not-very-slow Jeff Wilson. No try, but it showed how New Zealand could be beaten.

ALFRED ULUINAYAU

While rugby fans sat back and waited expectantly for the likes of Lomu and Cullen to electrify the World Cup, it was the unknown Fijian full back Alfred Uluinayau who grabbed the headlines in the narrow 28-19 pool match against France. Receiving the ball on halfway, Uluinayau set off at an unbelievable lick straight through a gap in the French defence, leaving even flyers Dominici and Bernat-Salles rooted to the spot. As a display of raw pace and finishing power, it was not beaten in the tournament.

BACKS

In today's game, where even fly halves are brick outhouses, there are still certain rugby players who are capable of breaking a defence with a moment of dazzling skill. Slippery as eels, you'd certainly want this lot on your World Cup sevens team.

The SLIPPERY VII

MARK ELLA

The Wallabies touring side of 1984 was one of the greatest ever to set foot in the British Isles. It contained future stars such as David Campese and Michael Lynagh, but the maestro who pulled the strings and singlehandedly revolutionised fly-half play was Mark Ella. On that tour, Ella used pace, sleight of hand, and acute tactical awareness to carve open each of the four Home Nations. He scored in each Test, set up countless others, and left crowds gobsmacked at his brilliance. Tragically for the game, he then retired at the ridiculously young age of 25.

WAISALE SEREVI

Even from a nation that breeds brilliant sevens players, Fijian maestro Waisale Serevi is the greatest ever. Unbelievable pace, awareness, handling skills, finishing power, cheekiness … the list goes on, yet it still does no justice to a man who takes the game of rugby to untold heights of brilliance. It is a shame, therefore, that there seems to be no place in the modern 15-a-side game for a player whose attacking genius is at the expense of a rugged defensive game. Had he been playing 25 years ago, he would have been a superstar at both sevens and fifteens.

ROY LAIDLAW

One half of the marvellous Rutherford-Laidlaw axis which dominated Scotland and the Five Nations during the 1980s, Roy Laidlaw was a combative No. 9 who appeared to be able to slice open defences at will. He never had great pace, but instead his natural eye for a break and a brilliant dummy were often enough to take him steaming through even the most congested defence from the base of the scrum.

TIM HORAN

Another Aussie attacking genius, Tim Horan proved in the 1999 World Cup that even rock solid modern defences can be ripped apart by pace, guile, and an eye for the gap. At the age of 29, Horan was deservedly voted Man of the Tournament and he played no better game than the semi-final against South Africa. Despite suffering from a bout of food poisoning, Horan cut the awesome Springbok midfield to ribbons with his lightning breaks.

PHIL BENNETT

Yes, we know 'Benny' already has a slot in the Ugly XV. But just to prove there are no hard feelings, we allow him to take his rightful pride of place in the Slippery VII. New Zealand would not disagree with our decision, having been side-stepped off the park by the Welsh fly half during the 1973 Barbarians game. Nor would the South Africans, who were ripped to shreds by Bennett's elusive genius during the Lions tour the following year. During a brilliant career, Bennett perfected not so much the side-step as the side-leap – to the embarrassment of opponents around the world.

RICHARD SHARP

Thirty years before Rob Andrew tamed the Five Nations with his boot, England actually had a fly half who could run rings around the opposition. Richard Sharp made his debut in 1960 against Wales, and led England to a rare win with his mesmeric running. He dominated the position for seven years, but it was against Scotland in 1965 that he recorded his finest performance. Not only did Sharp destroy the defence, he also scored one of the great tries by selling dummy after dummy as he threaded his way through the helpless Scottish tacklers.

PETER JACKSON

England winger Peter Jackson was once described as a cross between Nijinsky and Stanley Matthews, and there is no better way of summing up his genius. Quite simply, he had it all: handling, sidestep, pace. In tandem with Richard Sharp, he turned the English back line of the 1960s into a potent attacking threat – something they have not often achieved since. His finest hour was against the 1958 Wallabies, when in the dying seconds he eluded seven tackles to score the winning try of the match. It's a try that is still regarded as one of the greatest even today.

BACKS

The SOFT VII

Everyone who has ever turned out for their local third XV enjoys those special moments in top-class rugby when the so-called superstars prove that, deep down, they are as hopeless at tackling as you are. Here, then, are seven of the dodgiest...

GRANT FOX

With his pack steaming forward and his right boot working like a metronome, life was grand for New Zealand fly half Grant Fox. But on the rare occasion that the opposition got the ball and, more specifically, ran straight at him, the Kicking Machine was apt to turn into the Jelly. Of course, Fox would no doubt state regally that it was not his place to put the tackles in – but that was surely no excuse to avoid the exercise altogether.

LES CUSWORTH

Another leading member of the Non-Tackling Fly Half Union, Les's finest moment came in a match against Wales in 1988. After allowing his opposite number Jonathan Davies to make several unimpeded yards up the middle of the park, Cusworth was on hand a few moments later to completely bottle the crucial tackle on winger Adrian Hadley. As the Welshman strolled over the line to score the winning try, you could almost see him laughing at poor Les flat out on the Twickenham turf.

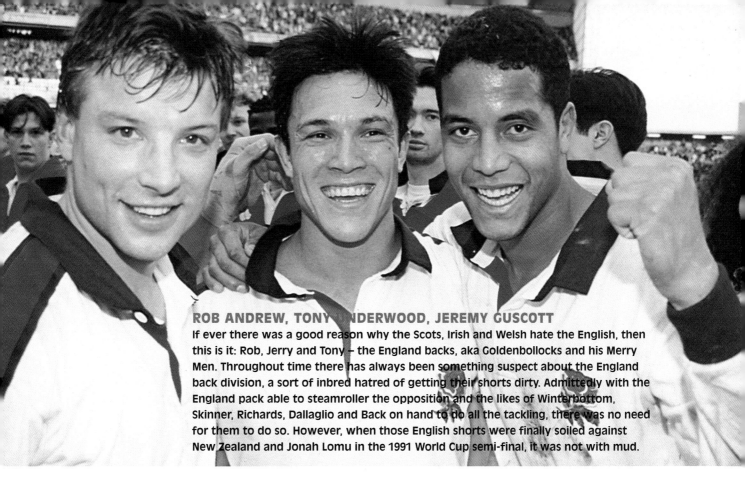

ROB ANDREW, TONY UNDERWOOD, JEREMY GUSCOTT

If ever there was a good reason why the Scots, Irish and Welsh hate the English, then this is it: Rob, Jerry and Tony – the England backs, aka Goldenbollocks and his Merry Men. Throughout time there has always been something suspect about the England back division, a sort of inbred hatred of getting their shorts dirty. Admittedly with the England pack able to steamroller the opposition and the likes of Winterbottom, Skinner, Richards, Dallaglio and Back on hand to do all the tackling, there was no need for them to do so. However, when those English shorts were finally soiled against New Zealand and Jonah Lomu in the 1991 World Cup semi-final, it was not with mud.

XAVIER GARBAJOSA

All right, nobody in their right minds would like to tackle Jonah Lomu. But then again, most of us are not highly-paid professional rugby players. Xavier Garbajosa is – and against Lomu in the World Cup semi-final of 1999, the French full back showed a quite extraordinary sidestep to get the hell out of the way of the rampaging winger as he bore down for his second try of the match. In the excitement of the match, Garbajosa's cowardice was forgotten. But not by us.

BARRY JOHN

Sorry, Barry. You might have been the world's greatest fly half, but when it came to tackling you were simply not at the races. These days, we only ever see the great tries that the King either scored or created. But it is worth watching those rare tries scored against Wales during his reign. Inevitably, John is nowhere to be seen, or else he is attempting to bring down his opponent with the puniest of slaps to the shorts.

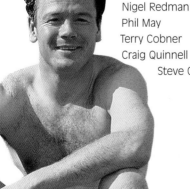

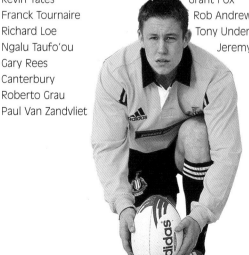

IF YOU ENJOYED THIS BOOK, YOU'LL GET A KICK OUT OF...

Bizarre Fantasy Football XI's is available at your local bookshop. Alternatively, it can be ordered direct from the publisher. Please send a cheque for £8.99 (£7.99 plus £1 for postage and packaging) to:
Generation Publications Ltd,
9 Holyrood Street,
London SE1 2EL.

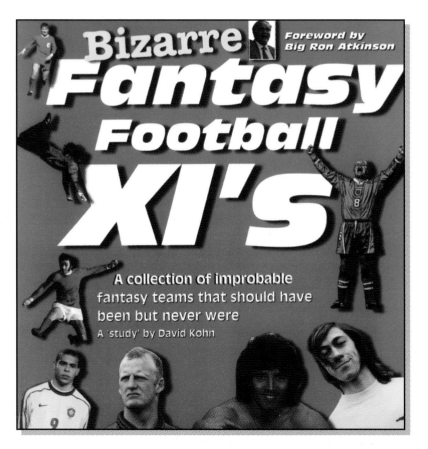